Tapping Your Secret Source of Power

Lee Buck
with Dick Schneider

Tapping Your Secret Source of Power

Fleming H. Revell Company
Old Tappan, New Jersey

Scripture quotations identified NEB are from The New English Bible. Copyright © The Delegates of the Oxford University Press and the Syndics of the Cambridge University Press 1961, 1970. Reprinted by permission.

Scripture quotations identified KJV are from the King James Version of the Bible.

Scripture quotations identified RSV are from the Revised Standard Version of the Bible, copyrighted 1946, 1952, © 1971 and 1973.

Material from *Seeds of Greatness* by Denis Waitley is copyright © 1983 by Denis E. Waitley, Inc. Used by permission of Fleming H. Revell Company.

We acknowledge with thanks permission to use excerpts or adaptations from the following copyrighted stories which were originally published in *Guideposts* magazine: "My Race Against Hate" by Mario Andretti; "On the Way Up" by Lee Buck; "Voyage" by Edward Carlson; "Hurry Before the Ice Cream Melts" by Tom Carvel; "There Are Winners and There Are Winners" by Rick Hamlin; "When I Wasn't Too Sure" by Julie Harris; "Moment of Decision" by William Lear; "Words to Grow On" by Pat O'Brien; "Getting There" by Donald Seibert; "Not Part of My Job" by Elisa Vazquez. Copyright © 1971, 1973, 1975, 1983, 1984 respectively by Guideposts Associated, Inc., Carmel, New York 10512. All rights reserved by Guideposts Associates, Inc.

"How I Found My Secret Source of Power" is based on material which appeared in *Voice* magazine, July 1984. Published by Full Gospel Business Men's Fellowship International, Costa Mesa, California.

Library of Congress Cataloging in Publication Data

Buck, Lee.
   Tapping your secret source of power.

   Bibliography: p.
   1. Success in business. 2. Interpersonal
relations. 3. Conduct of life. I. Schneider, Dick, date.
II. Title.
HF5386.B882 1985   650.1   85-2389
ISBN 0-8007-1422-9

TO my wife, Audrey,
and my four lovely daughters,
Melody, Merrilee, Bonnie, and Lisa.

This book is given as an offering of love and joy. But, most of all, this book is dedicated to those in the everyday working world who are seeking and unfulfilled, who live lives of stress, and who suffer that eternal loneliness that occurs without a source of power.

Contents

How This Book
Came About
by Dick Schneider

While browsing through a large bookstore in New York City's Fifth Avenue one sunny noon hour, I began to feel a sense of oppression. On looking around, I found myself besieged by a massive display of "success" books designed to teach me how to get mine, win by intimidation, look out for number one, and have it all as I gained success (!) and power (!).

In a way, I felt as if I were being stared down, elbowed aside, and stepped on by eager strivers who were out to win despite anything. Yet I knew that these principles seemed popular in today's world of "me first."

So, I picked up and looked at a few of these books.

Robert Ringer, author of *Looking Out for Number One*, advised me that I should look out chiefly for my own interests as I did my "primary moral duty." That "duty," according to Ringer, is to pursue pleasure, being careful, of course, not to "forcibly interfere with the rights of others."[1]

I picked up Michael Korda's *Success! How Every Man and Woman Can Achieve It* and was momentarily encouraged to see that Korda believes we all have a right to succeed and we shouldn't feel guilty about a perfectly natural ambition. *So far, so good,* I thought. But then along with telling me it is okay to be ambitious, have a good time, and be a winner, he added:

"It's O.K. to be greedy. . . .

"It's O.K. to be Machiavellian (if you can get away with it).

"It's O.K. to recognize that honesty is not always the best policy (provided you don't go around saying so).

"And it's *always* O.K. to be rich."[2]

I began to wonder. Whatever happened to morals and ethics? Korda seemed to have anticipated my concern, for he proceeded to tell me, *"How* you become a success is, of course, your business. Morality has very little to do with success."[3]

Korda does not believe it is necessary to be dishonest or unethical to succeed, but he advises the reader to be prepared for some tough infighting along the way, no matter what your ethics might be. Accept the rules of whatever game you have chosen and *play to win.*[4]

How do you play to win? To those climbing the corporate ladder Korda advises:

Nobody *expects* you to be 100 percent loyal at heart, but it is one of those values that must be publicly displayed if you're going to get ahead. . . . Nobody minds ruthless, egocentric careerism and self-interest, provided they are suitably screened. If you can undermine your boss and replace him, fine, do so, *but never express anything but respect and loyalty for him while you're doing it.*[5]

Suddenly, it all became too much for me. I fled the store, only to be confronted at the curb by the latest message from one of Manhattan's new advertising entrepreneurs who dash about the city at midnight spray-painting stenciled messages on the streets at crosswalks.

Staring up at me from the black asphalt were the freshly sprayed yellow words of a new book title: *Don't Get Mad . . . Get Even!*

After escaping into a taxi cab I flagged down, I opened my *New York Times* to be confronted by a business-page headline: "The Age of 'Me-First' Management."

"Many are alarmed that America's corporate chiefs are losing sight of moral standards in the new frenzy to get rich," observed reporter Ann Crittenden. She quoted Charles T. Munger, vice-chairman, Berkshire Hathaway Inc., Omaha, who, in testifying before a congressional subcommittee on corporate takeovers, said: "Look at the economy as a great stew. And look at those hostile takeover related activities, and all this related money-making with no risk by the Jay Gould types which are increasingly predominating the capital scene, and look at them as salt. In the old days, we had a minor amount of salt in the stew; and all of a sudden, somebody's pouring . . . more salt in the stew. . . ."[6]

It all seemed related to what I had been reading in the bookstore. And when the cab pulled up in front of my building I was relieved to retreat to my office and its comfortable atmosphere, where I write inspirational stories for *Guideposts* magazine about people who have overcome a problem, gained new hope, or have achieved some noteworthy success in their lives.

As I hung up my coat, my secretary reminded me that I had an interview scheduled that afternoon with Lee Buck, the senior vice-president of marketing for the New York Life Insurance Company.

I looked forward to it, for I have always enjoyed talking to men and women who have achieved a worthwhile career in the business world. And Lee Buck had certainly done this, heading one of the most productive divisions of a leading insurance company.

An hour later I stepped from a cab in front of the imposing sky-scraper of New York Life, which has stood at its Madison Avenue address for over fifty years.

On stepping into the marbled hall with its banks of elevators, I was directed to one that went to the top floor. I punched his floor button, settled back against the mahogany panel as the car whirred skyward, and reflected on my trip to the bookstore during lunch hour.

Was life nothing more than a climb to the top accentuated by getting toeholds on the faces of others? Was winning and succeeding so important I had to do it by intimidation as I looked out for number one and savored the prospect of having it all?

I thought of the man I would be seeing in a few moments. Lee Buck was a success; would he be like all the rest?

The elevator stopped; its doors slid open and I walked down the hall to Lee Buck's office. In his reception room a secretary ushered me over a thick carpet into Lee's workplace. As large as the living room in my home, its windows offered a panorama of New York City skyscrapers. Lee bounced from behind his desk, shook hands, and asked me to sit down.

"Well," he said, returning to his swivel chair and leaning back, hands clasped behind his head, "what would you like to talk about?"

"A lot of things," I answered, "but first I'd like to center in on what you feel is your formula for success, something we can tell others that will help them."

"Oh," he smiled, "that's easy." And he reached to a table behind him, saying, "I have a book here that helped me a lot."

Oh, no, I thought. *Will it be Ringer? Korda? Brown?*

But it wasn't. In fact, the ideas that Lee Buck shared with me that day were the very antithesis of Ringer, Korda, and their ilk. Lee Buck's "secret of success" comes from a different source of power. The book he gets his ideas from is a symposium of sorts, written by more than a dozen authors and containing principles that are as old as the pyramids and as fresh as every sunrise. Read on to discover what that book was and what its secrets are.

On the following pages I help Lee Buck speak in the first person to tell you his story. He shares the principles that have helped him, and tells why these principles will work for anyone willing to try them.

The Day It Worked
for Me
by Lee Buck

On an April afternoon in 1973, I was at my desk in the home office of the New York Life Insurance Company when a phone call came from the secretary of the chairman of the board.

"Mr. Buck," she said, "he would like to see you in fifteen minutes."

My hands shook slightly as I set down the receiver. I had been waiting for this call. Now, at last, I was going to be offered the post I'd been striving for: senior vice-president in charge of marketing.

I deserved the promotion. I knew that. For twenty years, ever since I'd joined the company, I'd worked hard. For that matter, I'd always worked hard. My father had died early in the Great Depression, and for six years in Flint, Michigan, my mother, younger brother, and I lived on welfare. When she could, my mother ironed for others, kept boarders, and worked her fingers to the bone trying to keep our family intact. She ended up running a beer parlor called the Indian Village. A corner of the tavern, walled off with plasterboard, became our home.

By the time I was thirteen, I was out making money any way

possible to help support my mother and brother. I found an old, battered saxophone under the bed and learned to play it for tips at the tavern. We formed a musical trio with my mother at the piano and my brother on drums. Later I played with local bands.

The fear of going hungry and of not having a place to sleep constantly haunted me. My brother and I wore hand-me-down work shirts and overalls to school and I was sure that the other kids snickered at us.

It was then that I had decided that if anything good were to happen to me I would have to do it myself. I worked my way through college and was studying for my doctoral degree at the University of Michigan when I went to work for New York Life as an insurance agent.

By then I had married and, even more eager to make good, advanced through many positions, vigorously reaching for the next rung on the ladder, and then the next. On the way up I'd moved my family a number of times, but now I was in New York, zone vice-president in charge of sales in the eastern United States.

In a few minutes, upstairs, the chairman of the board was undoubtedly going to make me senior vice-president over marketing. I would be in charge of all the firm's ten thousand insurance salesmen in the United States. It was the most important phase of our operation. I savored the prospect. Everyone knew I wanted it, and I felt sure that the chairman knew I was the best candidate.

I glanced at my watch: five minutes since the call. I quickly straightened the papers on my desk, rose, and told my secretary where I was going.

"Oh?" She raised her eyebrows. She knew that being called to see the chairman meant something very important.

I stepped briskly toward the stairwell. Usually when people went up to the chairman's office on the next floor they took the elevator. But that was a longer walk down the hall—a waste of time, I felt.

As I hurried toward the gray-painted steel door under the lighted EXIT sign, I thought how pleased my wife, Audrey, was going to be. She'd had a rough time because of our many moves, raising four daughters while I spent week after week on the road.

I pushed open the door, started to climb the steps . . . and then I stopped.

The thought of Audrey made me think of something else. It was a whole new way of looking at life and how its turns and changes affect us. It had completely turned around my usual reaction to life's exigencies. Only a few years earlier I would have thoroughly ridiculed the idea. Now, I was employing it more and more.

I called it tapping my secret source of power.

Actually, the idea was not new. It has been used for thousands of years by people who have achieved success. I'll try to explain it simply. In any conflict or change there is the potential for both pain and good, as with fire, which can hurt and destroy, or comfort and illuminate. Thus, instead of fighting or chafing at the situation, if one seeks the inherent good and surrenders to it, he or she is endowed with the perspective to act on that good for the benefit of everyone concerned. The will to act on that good comes from your power source.

As you read this book you will see the concept at work in a variety of ways.

At the time of the 1973 meeting with my firm's chairman of the board, tapping my power source was still a new revelation to me. And though I had employed it in small ways up until then, I had never staked my career on it.

No matter what happened in the chairman's office, would I dare do it now?

For a long moment I stood in the stairwell, grasping the stair rail, coming to a decision. Yes, I finally decided, now would be the time. I looked up and drew a deep breath. The relaxed feeling inside me was for real. My heart settled and I walked up the stairs and then out into the hall and down to the chairman's office.

"Go right in, Mr. Buck," said the chairman's secretary. "He's expecting you."

I stepped into the large, carpeted room where heavy drapes at the windows muted the sound of traffic on Madison Avenue. The gray-haired man behind the massive mahogany desk leaned across it and shook my hand. He motioned me to a chair. Slowly, he turned a paperweight in his hands, over and over. He stood, walked to a window, then turned to me and said, "Lee, I'm going to ask you a question and I don't want you to jump out of your chair when I ask it."

"I'm not going to jump out of my chair," I said with a smile. "What do you want?"

He sat down at his desk and expelled the words rapidly. "We want you to run the group marketing department. We're going to make George senior vice-president in charge of marketing. And we'll make you senior vice-president over group marketing. Will you do it?"

I stared at him. Group department? In my mind it was a real comedown. This division, which sold group policies to companies and organizations, did only about a fifth of the business that marketing accounted for and had only a fraction of the number of personnel.

I felt a surge of disappointment and anger. But only for a moment. I leaned back in my chair and smiled. "Okay," I said.

He stared at me, astonished. Obviously he had been expecting a different reaction from me. He was well aware of my feisty reputation. "Do . . . do you really mean that?" he asked.

"Isn't that what you want me to do?"

"Yes, it is."

"Well, then," I said, "let's go."

Then and there we started talking about my new duties, and I was alert and excited. Once upon a time I would have been too disappointed to even feign enthusiasm, but now, ten minutes after my voluntary surrender, I was a secure man, even ready for what seemed like bad news.

At that time, the group department was considered something of a stepchild in the company. In the eyes of my co-workers, I had been pushed aside. Some agents even came to me and offered their condolences. When I said I looked forward to the opportunity, they thought I was putting up a front.

In odd ways, I could tell that I had lost prestige in the company. At Christmastime, for instance, when I used to get hundreds of greeting cards, the number now dropped dramatically. All in all, these things taught me something. Prestige and stature in the business world—what so many people struggle for—have as much substance as a mist that soon evaporates. I was discovering again a vital power greater than myself.

Meanwhile, I had a job to do, and soon I truly believed that it was not only an opportunity but a *great* opportunity.

I remembered the advice of a very successful veteran insurance agent when I had asked for his sales secret. "Jump at every opportunity, son," he answered in his usual laconic way.

"But how do I recognize the opportunities?" I pressed.

"You can't," he smiled, "you have to keep jumping."

It was advice that has never failed me. And so I started jumping.

Stimulated as I had never been before, I threw myself into the challenge. In studying our market potential, we found new prospects that had not been contacted before. Our sales force became inspired and everyone really went at it, calling on banks, teachers' associations, and business groups that had never been approached. I myself went out and made hundreds of sales calls. By the first year we had sold $75 million in new premiums, about double what the department had done the previous year.

And so we all kept jumping, attending every trade-association meeting, getting out there and trying. One of these meetings led us to a prospect. It took many months of discussion in showing him how our policy would help his association, but it paid off. He finally ordered the largest single new premium ever written by our company.

It was fun.

Almost five years went by. Then one afternoon, I received a call from the chairman of the board. Once more I felt the butterflies as I left for his office. And once more I stopped on the stair landing to reaffirm that whatever strength I needed would come from my power source.

Then I walked into the chairman's office. "Lee," he said, "I have some good news for you." He walked over and shook my hand. "We want you to be senior vice-president in charge of marketing."

"That's wonderful," I said calmly.

He looked at me quizzically. I knew he thought I should be more excited. "Isn't that what you always wanted?"

"Is that what you want me to do?"

"Of course," he said.

"Well, then," I said, "let's go!"

For five years Lee Buck distinguished himself as senior vice-president in charge of marketing for New York Life. He helped set new sales records and earned numerous awards in capping a distinguished career of over thirty-four years. In 1983, he retired to devote himself to helping others discover their secret source of power. The principles outlined in this book are designed to help the reader tap into that source.

The Butterfly Effect

Weathermen speak of the "Butterfly Effect"—the idea that a butterfly flapping its wings today in Peking might affect the weather next month in New York.

They base this on a phenomenon that physicists call "sensitive dependence on initial conditions," the fact that tiny differences in input could become overwhelming differences in output.

The same principle applies, I believe, to the little things we do or say today having an overwhelming effect on our future.

As the old saying goes, *What you are to be, you are now becoming.* And you can gain a measure of insight and control over the Butterfly Effects in your life if you learn how to tap your secret source of power. This book will show you how.

Tapping Your
Secret Source
of Power

—1—
The Principle of Putting Others First

Normally, I am not a bumper-sticker person, but I couldn't help but notice the message of the Chevrolet Camaro ahead of me: ME FIRST, YOU SECOND. In less than half a mile, the driver's attitude was put into practice to its extreme. The Camaro passed the car ahead of it as they rounded a curve, narrowly missing a Honda traveling in the opposite direction. Amid horn blasting and fist shaking, the driver of the Camaro sped away, apparently unperturbed, and satisfied that, for now, at least, he was in the lead.

I used to believe in the "Me first, you second" school of thought, but in time I had to ask myself, what does that kind of life get you but ulcers and hypertension, not to mention highway accidents?

"You're a Good Insurance Man, Lee, But. . . ."

In my early days in the life insurance business, there was one person I was working for: Lee Buck. Oh, sure, I told myself I was trying to provide security for my wife and little girls. But basically it was, "Get out there and get mine." The more policies I sold the more my ego was gratified. The more I accomplished, the higher standing I felt I had in the eyes of others. Selling more and larger policies and being promoted in the company were my ultimate goals. After all, I reasoned, wasn't that what work was all about?

I began learning there was a different answer from an older agent who accompanied me on my first rounds. He would sit back and listen as I discussed policies with a prospect.

One evening we pulled up to a small house in a poor neighborhood. A young man with tired eyes met us at the door. He had inquired about insurance. When I saw his wife lead three little children to bed and learned this couple had bought their house on a mortgage only three years ago, I could well understand his concern about providing for his family if something happened to him.

In my presentation I pulled out all stops in attempting to convince the young husband that he would show love for his family in no better way than by purchasing a substantial amount of insurance.

After looking over the figures, the man slowly shook his head. "Let me think about it," he said. I was about to remind him that fate is capricious, that too many men had left this world while "thinking about it," when the older agent caught my eye and indicated it was time to leave. As we drove home he proceeded to give me a lecture about selling insurance.

"Lee, you put the cart before the horse. Instead of trying to get your name on the company president's list, you should be thinking of the needs and capabilities of that poor guy back there who gets up at five o'clock every morning to put in a heavy day at the assembly plant."

I was glad it was dark so the agent couldn't see my face flame. He was quiet for a moment, sensing that he had cut deep. Then he continued.

"You're a good insurance man, Lee. I can see that and you'll go far. But you'll go further if you can remember to put the other guy first, do everything you can to insure his welfare.

"And I can guarantee," he added quietly, "that you'll get a lot more satisfaction out of your work."

This was one of many learning steps in my profession. Later, I returned to that plant worker and in finding out about his needs was able to work out a starter policy that fit his budget. Though it wouldn't support his family for long, it would preserve his home if he died.

But it wasn't until later that I fully understood the wisdom in the older agent's advice to "put the other guy first." Suppose he had let me convince that young father to purchase a large policy? I might have enjoyed a momentary glow of success as I counted the bigger commission, but what might have happened down the line? Some young people load themselves down with unrealistic insurance policies, only to drop them when their budgets get tight. A smaller policy or term insurance of some kind is more apt to be retained, and to *be there* when needed. In this case, my client had no trouble paying for the smaller policy and later, when he was financially able, he contacted me about buying more insurance.

I realize that's a nice little story that illustrates how looking out for your customers' needs pays off in the end. But I have come to see that the principle of putting others first has many other applications. For example, sometimes putting the other guy first is as simple as doing the best job you can because that's what you're being paid for. Another secret of success is to give it all you've got, even when it doesn't look as if there will be much of a payoff.

The Actor Who Played It With All He Had

Take the case of a little-known actor who was barely making a living back in 1930. His future looked bleak. In fact, the Broadway play in which he had a role was about to fold. It was called *The Up and Up.* One of its scenes left the young man completely exhausted after he played it. That was because the scene called for him to argue with two angry men, one perched on the edge of his desk and the other on the phone. Afterward, he was soaked with perspiration from putting so much of himself into it. Despite everything, the play itself got mixed reviews. It moved to a less prestigious theater, the actors accepted less pay, but the handwriting was on the wall.

Under these doleful circumstances, the young actor was

tempted to coast through the scene. After all, he reasoned, why knock himself out on something that was hopeless?

Then something he'd heard ever since his boyhood days came back to him: "Whatever task lies to your hand, do it with all your might. . . ."[1] So the young actor stuck with it. He continued to put everything he had into that scene. And almost every time he did it he found himself wondering, *What's the use? Nobody cares that much anyway.*

Finally the play folded and the young man moved on to other small plays. Then one winter day, over a year later, he got a surprising phone call. It was from a representative of Howard Hughes, who was making movies at the time.

"Mr. Hughes is filming the play *The Front Page,*" said the caller, "and he wants you in it."

At first the young man thought someone was pulling his leg. But finally he was convinced and within a few days was aboard the Twentieth Century Limited heading for Hollywood. His role in the film *The Front Page* launched him to stardom. But why he had been selected to play that part was a mystery to him. It was Lewis Milestone, director of *The Front Page,* who finally revealed to him how it all came about.

"I was in New York last year and some friends and I had a block of seats for a hit Broadway show," Milestone explained. "We were one seat short so I volunteered to step across the street to another theater. It was presenting *The Up and Up* and plenty of seats were available. *The Up and Up* wasn't much of a play but one scene really impressed me. It was the one with the big argument and I could see you put everything you had into it. When we started doing this movie it called for a similar scene but we couldn't get anybody to do it right. Then I remembered the night I saw you in *The Up and Up* and that's why we called."

The Front Page launched that young actor on a fabulous movie career, but Pat O'Brien always remembered that what really got him started was what kept him going back when he had a role in a play that was a flop. O'Brien practiced the simple secret of doing his best, even when it didn't seem to matter.

As somebody said, "You never know who's watching." It can be a prospective buyer, employer, or associate. Of course, it can be someone you'll never see again. In Pat O'Brien's case, his efforts produced a tremendous payoff, but the idea of doing your best doesn't work on a tit-for-tat, quid-pro-quo basis. It's not as simple as saying, "I'll do things right because I know there will be a payoff." The benefits—if there are any—evolve over a period of time. Sometimes it can take years.

It Was Only a $2,500 Policy

Arthur Ginn, a New York Life insurance agent in Palatka, Florida, will attest to that. As a new agent he had been working with a young husband who had difficulty deciding what type of policy to buy. Finally, Arthur was able to convince him that at this time a $2,500 policy would be best.

Before he signed for it, however, a representative from another insurance firm stepped into the picture. He offered the prospect what appeared to be a policy with similar coverage at lower cost.

When Arthur learned this from his prospect, he was tempted to cross it all off his list. After all, even then, a $2,500 policy was small potatoes. Why waste more time with someone who was about to sign with another firm?

However, Arthur felt that he owed the young man something, especially if he was going to handle his job with all his "might." "Just what kind of policy are you being offered?" he asked the young man. He sat down with him and carefully went over both policies. He discovered that though the competitor's policy was lower in initial cost, it would end up costing more over its term. Patiently he explained this; he did not have to denigrate his competition. A factual comparison of the two policies was enough to convince the young man that Arthur Ginn's plan was better for him.

He purchased the $2,500 policy. Two years later he bought another one. As he became more successful in business, he turned to Arthur Ginn, a man he felt he could trust, again and again. Today that prospect, now a middle-aged man, owns several million dollars' worth of insurance, all of it purchased through Arthur Ginn, all of it because Arthur Ginn cared enough to give of himself without thought of recompense.

Arthur Ginn is the first one to minimize his efforts. To him, it was "just part of the job," a job, by the way, which he enjoys immensely. And this is another benefit when one truly puts the other person first: He or she reaps a fierce enjoyment out of work.

Just a Little Neighborhood Drugstore

One way to sum up everything we've been saying so far is to put it in familiar words that we often hear: It is more blessed to give than to receive.[2] A young farm boy from northern Illinois discovered this in a surprising way at the turn of the century. He had traveled to Chicago to find a job and build a career. But success, even plain satisfaction, did not come easily. In fact, the boy held several jobs as a drug clerk in various stores, but none promised that big opportunity.

Finally, he landed a job with a druggist on Chicago's South Side. But still it wasn't the job of which he had dreamed. Besides, he didn't like his boss's attitude and felt he was too much of a taskmaster. So he decided to quit. But then he thought, why make it easy for his employer to hire a better clerk?

So he set his heart on doing the very best job he could. After a few weeks of this, he would leave. Then, wouldn't the boss be sorry to lose him?

The young clerk was in for a surprise. The store owner, noticing the sudden improvement, gave him a raise. The clerk took it as a challenge. He worked even harder and got another raise. Soon he began to study pharmacy at night.

In 1901 he purchased his own drugstore, just a little neighborhood store on Chicago's South Side. There was nothing about it that was different from the hundreds of other drugstores serving the city.

By this time the young proprietor had learned the secret of doing his best while putting others first. His work became fun. As a result, customers noticed something extra that wasn't on the shelves or in the display window—a certain spirit. For the pharmacist felt that if shoppers were made to feel important, more people would continue to trade with him.

One of his favorite devices was used when a customer phoned in for an order to be delivered. While he talked with the person on the phone, he would signal a helper and repeat the order loud and clear. While he engaged the customer in pleasantries, the helper would package the order and hustle out the door to his bicycle. On occasion the customer would interrupt the phone conversation with the pharmacist to say: "Oh, excuse me, there's someone at my door." And, of course, she would be flabbergasted to find her order waiting.

The pharmacist's enthusiasm inspired his staff. Soon he opened a second store, then a third. Eventually, they became the largest chain of drugstores in the United States in sales. The proprietor? Charles R. Walgreen, Sr.

It All Depends on Who You're Working For

To practice putting others first, you need to answer a question: "Just *who* am I working for—myself or others?"

The dog-eat-dog approach says, "Why, I'm working for myself, of course, doesn't everybody?"

A modified version of the dog-eat-dog philosophy usually sounds like this: "I'm working for my family, to provide for my spouse and kids." The focus is still on *me* and *mine*.

Putting others first focuses on *them* and *theirs*. It sounds impractical, even foolhardy, but oddly enough, the more you practice the principle of others first, the more satisfaction and real success you have.

For one man, the turning point came in 1946, not long after he returned from service in World War II. Married, with a baby girl, his little family was in financial need and he desperately sought any kind of work.

He was offered a summer job playing piano with a small orchestra at a resort on Chautauqua Lake in New York State. Taking his family, he traveled to the lake, where he joined the other band members. For living quarters, the group leased rooms near the pavilion where they would be playing. Their landlord supported his own family by renting these rooms along with summer cottages. All went well until midsummer when a cold rain lashed the area and the weather settled into dismal gray days that kept customers away. Business got so bad that the pavilion owner couldn't pay the band "until things got better."

The landlord said he would wait for his rent until business picked up. But the cold rain persisted and it didn't look as if things would improve.

One by one, the band members slipped away at night. "Got to look out for number one," was the common excuse.

Finally, the piano player, his wife and baby were the only ones left.

What should he do? There was still the rent on all the rooms to be paid.

It didn't take him long to decide, because he had already answered a more important question. He approached the landlord and offered to work for him to pay off the lease. The surprised man was only too glad to agree to those arrangements.

The piano player worked hard—cleaning cottages, changing beds, and washing sheets. He also worked at a nearby grape juice processing plant. It was rough work, wrestling the heavy canvas filters from the grape presses and washing them.

Finally, he was able to pay off the balance owed on the lease. The landlord had tears in his eyes. "It wasn't the money," he said later, "as much as knowing that there were still people in the world who were as good as their word."

Not long after that, the young husband got a job as a shoe clerk with a J. C. Penney store in Bradford, Pennsylvania. He made his way from assistant store manager, to manager, and on up the corporate ladder. In 1974, Donald Seibert became chairman of the board of the J. C. Penney Company, leading his firm to new heights until his retirement in 1984.

Donald Seibert is still busy today. He heads the National Retailing Federation, and still finds time to serve diligently in his church in New Jersey. He has found a major secret to enjoying life: *You first, me second.*

Summing Up

The Principle of Putting Others First

1. Putting yourself first is always a short-range view.

2. Putting others first guarantees the most satisfaction for everyone in the long run.

3. Quid pro quo (something for something) is not the real motive for putting others first.

4. Whatever you have to do, give it all you have.

5. You never know who may be watching.

6. Decision making is easier if you have already made putting others first a rule for living.

7. For review at the end of each working day: "Who am I really working for?"

—2—
The Principle of Turning the Other Shoulder Blade

It was one of those casual comments tossed out during a business lunch which wisdom bade me ignore but ego would not let pass. A friend from another department, grousing about an office situation, took a sip of his tea, set down the cup, and sighed: "Guess we just have to expect it, Lee. People say things about everybody, it seems—about me, about you—"

"About me?" I interjected, putting down my fork and staring at him. "What's being said about me?"

He shook his head ruefully. "I'm sorry, Lee. It's all a lot of office crap. I shouldn't have mentioned it."

By now, my chicken chow mein had solidified in my stomach. "Come on, Michael," I demanded, "give it to me straight. If somebody's been gossiping about me, I want to know about it."

Michael moved the fried rice around on his plate with his fork. "Well, if you must know, Fred Lancer has been saying that you're so burned at not getting that divisional management post he took over that you're popping off to everybody about it." Michael stared at the rice he had piled into a little pyramid. "He also says you couldn't handle it, anyway."

My temples throbbed and I saw red, and it wasn't the Chinese lacquered wall behind my lunch partner.

How rotten can a guy get? I thought. It was true that I was in line for that divisional management post which Fred Lancer had taken over. But I hadn't said a word about it, even though I knew that Lancer, an older man who had been demoted from a similar post a few years ago, was not as qualified for it as I was. But I had not complained to anyone. To have done so would have been openly admitting my hurt, something I would not have revealed to anyone. But now, his passing around this guff rubbed salt in an open wound.

"It's a lie, Michael," I said, wiping my mouth with a napkin and standing up to leave. "I never said a word about it."

"I know," he said, fumbling with his coat, "but you know Lancer."

Yes, I knew Lancer. He knew how badly I wanted that job and in putting himself into my place he probably assumed I would be backbiting him. But I hadn't said a word.

All that afternoon I brooded about it and that night at dinner I blew off to my wife, Audrey. Audrey tried to calm me down, and even gave me some advice based on what she'd been hearing at the church she had been attending—alone. I'd been too busy to go with her; besides, if anyone needed preaching to it was Fred Lancer, not me.

That night I had trouble getting to sleep. It was bad enough not getting the job I should have been given, but having the guy who got it slander me was more than I could take.

It came to a head one night at a company party at a country club. Some of the men were clustered about in groups laughing and talking. I was with one group when I happened to look up and see Fred Lancer standing by himself at a window. He was glaring at me, so I decided I had better get the situation out into the open. I walked over to him. He raised his glass and grunted: "Sorry, you feel the way you do, ol' man."

Anger flared within me. "What are you talking about, Fred?"

Squinting at me over his glass, he snarled, "You know what I'm talking about, hotshot; you're burned up because you didn't get that divisional post when you're still wet behind the ears. Why don't you grow up and quit bellyaching about it?"

My fists clenched. "That's not so; I never said a thing!"

Slamming his glass down on a table, he leaned his florid face into mine. "You calling me a liar?"

Right then I wanted to slug him in the stomach as hard as I could.

"Just start something, buddy," I said quietly.

For a long moment we faced each other. Then I broke the spell. "Whoever said I was shooting my mouth off about that job is a liar, Fred. I never mentioned anything about it."

He picked up his glass, drained it, and walked off.

Our paths did not cross for a long while after that. I advanced into another division, earned some promotions, and four years later became a regional vice-president.

The post put me in charge of all divisional managers including—yes—Fred Lancer.

Now I had him. The temptation, of course, was to lean on him with everything I had. It happens all the time in the business world. If you cross someone, they'll repay you down the line. "Forgive and forget" is for fairy tales and fools. So now I had my chance to practice the code of revenge. I could lean on Fred Lancer so hard he would rue the day he ever slandered me or anyone else. But I didn't. Fortunately, by then I had learned a secret I like to call, "When you're stabbed in the back, turn the other shoulder blade." I had discovered that people are not my enemies—only misunderstandings and wrong thoughts are.

Fred Lancer was not my enemy. I could even understand his reasoning behind the accusations he'd made to me years before. Insecure about his own position, he transferred his fears to me. He expected me to speak ill about him and thus assumed that I had.

And so when I moved into that regional vice-presidency I determined to make Fred Lancer a friend, not a scapegoat or an example. I figured this was part of my job. And the only way to do it, I felt, was to become his friend. Real friendship isn't easy, especially in business. You have to give up a measure of power, probably the most coveted commodity in any company. But by then I had decided that type of power wasn't something I needed.

Oh, you can get burned; you can even get kicked in the teeth for your trouble. I had had both happen to me, but I still wanted to take the risk. So, whenever Fred Lancer needed to get something through the company, a clearance on a new policy formulation, or another plan to advance a sale, I made certain it was facilitated. I stood behind his decisions, and did everything to expedite them. Fred Lancer was a good insurance man and I determined to help him become even better.

Instead of ill will, I showed him kindness. Instead of demanding that he toe the mark in all those subtle ways a vice-president can use, I kept asking in different ways, "Is there anything I can do to help?" At first Fred was suspicious. He was trying to figure out how much rope I was trying to give him before he would hang himself. But as the months went on he sensed that the rope just wasn't there.

I believe everyone can eventually sense it when he's being treated with love and understanding. There is a current in the air that people respond to even if they can't explain it. A herd of wildebeests in Africa will be alert and worrisome, if a lion is in the vicinity, even if they don't see or sniff him. But if they know deep down they are safe, they graze with serenity.

Fred Lancer sensed the peaceful atmosphere between us. Neither of us ever mentioned our earlier problems. And he, in his own way, showed me he wanted to be a friend in return. After buying a house in the country, he stopped by my office one afternoon. "Hey, Lee," he said, "my wife and I would like you and Audrey to see our new place. Would you come for the weekend?" He was hesitant, as if half expecting me to say we had something else on for that weekend.

"Why, sure, Fred," I said. "We'd be delighted." It turned out to be a thoroughly pleasant visit.

In the years following, Fred turned out to be one of the best contributors to the region. But my biggest surprise came one night at a company banquet when I heard another piece of gossip. It was during the preliminaries, before we gathered for dinner, when Michael, the same man who first told me Fred Lancer had been talking behind my back, motioned me over. He was grinning. "Lee, I heard something I have to pass on to you."

I looked at him warily, remembering the last time he had something to "pass on."

"It's Fred Lancer, Lee," he said.

"Oh?"

"Yeah." Michael leaned close, obviously relishing what he was going to say. "Fred is telling everybody that if they need help from someone in the home office, the guy to count on is Lee Buck."

As someone once said, the wisest thing one can do to an enemy is to make him your friend. "Turning the other cheek" is hard enough to do when someone comes at you head-on and belts you one with a nasty word or deed. But turning the other shoulder blade when you get stabbed in the back carries the idea a few steps further. Earlier in my career it would have been natural to put Fred Lancer down once I got the opportunity. He would have been hurt, but so would I. For there is an elemental law that is as sure as gravity: *If you put someone down, you sink right along with him.*

Make Peace, Not War

It's easy to seek revenge; it's hard to seek an understanding. When you cross someone or someone crosses you, things can get out of hand, as this true story demonstrates. I have a friend who knows Mario Andretti, the famed racing driver. The story starts back in 1964 when Andretti was a twenty-four-year-old newcomer to auto racing. By that year the legendary champion driver A. J. Foyt was considered almost unbeatable on the racing circuit. But Andretti, brash and ambitious, was determined to beat him. In their first race together, a thirty-lap sprint at Allentown Fair in Pennsylvania, Foyt accidentally bumped Andretti's left front wheel, which caused him to spin out.

From then on, in Andretti's view, at least, he and Foyt were fierce rivals. Hot competition breeds gossip and soon "friends" were passing derogatory remarks supposedly made to one of the drivers by the other. "Most of this was pure bunk," commented Andretti later, "but it did the devil's work, stirring the fires of our personal enmity." Honest competition is healthy, but personal animosity can make it vicious.

It reached the point where the two would not speak to each other when passing in a hallway. Worse, the silent antagonism spilled over onto the raceway to the point where they were bumping wheels and cutting each other off. A wheel bump at 130 miles per hour can be deadly. This sort of vendetta can kill one or both of the participants.

Friends were concerned for both of them. Finally, the two drivers had a showdown. It took place at the DuQuoin Fair race in Illinois in 1966. Andretti and Foyt were at the prerace drivers' meeting, avoiding each other. Suddenly, Andretti looked up to see Foyt standing alone.

"From somewhere deep within myself," says Andretti, "came the conviction that it was wrong to let rivalry turn into bitterness. I knew we should not be enemies."

Somebody had to end it, he felt. So he stepped over to Foyt. "Maybe we should talk," Andretti said.

The two walked out to the parking lot behind the building. A hot Illinois sun beat down on the asphalt and in the distance a racing car rumbled in warm-up. The two stood there and talked openly, frankly.

They didn't say a whole lot, just talked objectively about their situation, without anger.

"We admitted to a mutual love—racing," said Andretti. "And we knew that if we kept going the way we were we would divide our world into two camps. We decided that it benefited neither of us to nurse a grudge."

That's all there was to it. They had cleared the air, and the two walked out of the parking lot together, free of a deadly burden.

It did not stop either of them from going all out for first place on the track. Both are great drivers. But without personal animosity they were able to race wheel to wheel and not worry.

As Andretti said afterward to my friend: "There's something in the Bible that says if two men have a bone to pick with each other, one should go to the other and talk it over with him in private.[1] Once we started talking, the rest was easy."

The key, of course, was *starting*. Andretti could have continued claiming that Foyt had stabbed him in the back and vice versa. They could have carried their grudge to the brink of disaster and beyond. But Andretti chose to quit nursing pride and start talking and trying to communicate. And to do that, he had to tap his power source.

A Time to Be Silent

The story of how Andretti and Foyt settled their 130-mile-an-hour feud nicely illustrates the value in openly confronting a problem and solving it one-on-one. But are there other instances when possibly the best thing to do when being "stabbed in the back" is simply be quiet and wait? I believe there are, and Dick Taylor would agree. Dick learned about the value of silence not long after he joined a New York City corporation as a department head.

The trouble began when he asked an assistant supervisor in another department to perform a minor service for a customer. It involved a mutual project in which both departments were involved, and it appeared to be in line with company policy.

The following day the head of the assistant supervisor's department strode into Dick Taylor's office to brusquely snap: "We don't do things like that!" Then he left.

Dick sat at his desk, dumbfounded. What could he have done wrong? As he was still new to the job, he thought the best thing to do was check the file involving the project. On opening it, he was set further back on his heels. In it was a note scribbled by the assistant supervisor to the man who had just castigated him. The note sarcastically referred to his request with a snappish comment as to why she felt it should not be done.

Taylor felt his head roaring as he read the note. Thrusting it back into the file, he glanced at the clock; the office was closing. Tomorrow, he vowed—tomorrow he would have it out with both of them. He had enough clout with the firm to make it rough on the woman he felt had caused the trouble.

All the way home his commuter-train wheels seemed to click out the words: hate, hate, hate. He couldn't enjoy dinner with his family and sat morosely in the living room, staring out the window. Even after his wife and children went to bed he stayed there, glowering into the dark, planning his revenge.

Later that night, while he lay in bed in a half-awake state, something kept running through his mind. He had been a churchgoer for years and prayed regularly. Now he just couldn't get a certain sentence out of his thoughts: "Forgive us our trespasses as we forgive those who trespass against us."[2]

No! he thought. *I could never forgive her.* Then it was as if a voice gently nudged him and said, *You've been forgiven your sins; can't you forgive someone else's?*

Taylor kept tossing and turning as he argued with the voice within. Finally he gave up and said, "All right, I can't handle this anymore. I'll forgive her."

Suddenly, as Taylor relates the story, a heavy weight seemed to lift from his body. He felt free and totally relaxed. With a light heart he settled down for a refreshing night's sleep.

The next morning he apologized to his family for his dark mood the previous evening. On the train he logically and unemotionally reviewed the entire situation involving his request, the woman, and her department head.

What caused her to write that note? he asked himself. He tried to see things from her position. Slowly he began to see that she could have misunderstood his request. *But why didn't she come to me?* he wondered. And the answer seemed given to him: It was obvious she was a very insecure person. Fearful of confronting someone in another department, she defensively wrote the note to her own department head who, Dick had already learned from office gossip, had a reputation of shooting first and asking questions afterward.

No matter, he thought to himself, he had forgiven her. He did remind himself, however, to stay clear of that particular assistant supervisor in the future.

But it didn't happen that way.

Dick's office was near the building's main entrance. And who should be the first person to come tripping by his door that very morning? Right. The woman.

Glancing into his office, she gave him a cheery smile: "Good morning, Dick!"

It was sincere, and he couldn't help but smile and respond, "Good morning."

There was something different about her, he could tell. She appeared brighter, happier. And her greeting seemed genuine.

As Taylor sat at his desk, thinking about his encounter with the woman, he smiled and shook his head. The note she had written yesterday had been a hurried response, after a long and frustrating day. Obviously, she had forgotten all about it.

But what would have happened if I hadn't kept quiet? Taylor thought. *What if I'd blown my cool at her last night?*

Dick knew the answer. It would have been a major confrontation in the office between his fellow department head and this employee and himself. And, in view of the circumstances involved, no one would have come out ahead. It would have been a virulent confrontation with a fallout that would have adversely affected a number of people.

How did it all eventually turn out? Dick, the woman, and her department head worked together happily and peaceably at the same office for twelve years. Nothing like that hasty note ever happened again. In fact, the woman became a very helpful colleague. Eventually she left the firm and now, years later, when she happens to meet Dick on Manhattan streets, she greets him warmly and effusively.

What happened the night that Dick Taylor abandoned his plan for hate and revenge? Was it supernatural? Was it a higher power? Or was it simply psychological? Did Taylor's superego simply prick his conscience and remind him of how he should act because he was a decent fellow?

I believe it was some of each. Whatever happened when Dick Taylor decided to give up and forgive, a powerful principle was at work, a principle just as valid as the law of physics which states that every action has its opposite and equal reaction. I believe that when Dick Taylor surrendered his hatred and desire for revenge that night, he loosened the bindings that made that woman his adversary. He simply released the whole situation into the positive realm of love.

By the same token, I am certain that if he had "bound" his adversary in the chains of hate and anger, he would have entrapped himself and all those around him in the netherworld of hopelessness, strife, and tragedy.

And a Time to Speak Up

While remaining silent may be the right thing to do under certain circumstances, it does not apply to all situations. As we can see with Dick Taylor, "biting his tongue" was far better than biting off his colleague's head. In other cases, though, it is necessary for people to be open and frank with each other. They don't have to bite off each others' heads, but they do need to clear the air. Too many evils fester under the cover of "Let's not make waves," or, "I guess I had better be polite."

The best lesson I ever received on being open and frank was taught to me by Allen Smith, an older executive in our company. One afternoon as I was returning from lunch, Allen stopped me in the hall. "Lee," he said, "could you come to my office later this afternoon?"

"Of course," I said, wondering what was on his mind. We had always been friends and from the tone of his voice he had a serious concern.

Later, during our talk, I found out just how serious. After the usual small talk, Allen leaned forward in his chair and studied his fingers, which he had folded tentlike before him.

"Lee," he began, "I have difficulty bringing this up, but I feel I must." He glanced at me, almost helplessly, and continued. "I've been told that you have been criticizing me and my operations to others."

I sat there aghast. His statement was incredible. This man whom I had always respected—me, malign him behind his back?

"Allen," I answered, looking at him straight, "you know I'd

never do that. If we did have problems, you know I'd come straight to you."

I knew Allen was a man of strong faith and self-confidence, so I continued, "We both love this company, Allen, and all I can tell you is that you have my word I never said such things."

Allen regarded me silently for a minute, then smiled in relief, stood up, and extended his hand. "Thanks, Lee. I believe you. I knew you wouldn't do anything like that, but I just needed to hear you say it."

A week later he asked me to lunch. I learned the rest of the story. "I went straight to the fellow who told me that story," he said, "and confronted him about it. 'Did you hear Lee say those things?' I asked him.

"The guy hesitated and said, 'Well, no, not really, but. . . .'

" 'Well, then,' I pressed, 'who *did* you hear it from?' "

Allen took a sip of coffee and smiled at me. "Well, Lee, the fellow waffled so much it soon became obvious that it was a figment of his imagination—a figment, I'm afraid," Allen shot me a rueful look, "of his trying to make himself look better by putting someone else in a bad light."

I sat there staring into my coffee. It happens so often: A person tries to build himself up by running someone else down.

The odd thing about it was that the maligner ended up working for me a year later. I said nothing about the incident to him; I felt certain he was suffering enough already. He was a very insecure man who seemed to look at life negatively, leaning more on office politics than on his own creative efforts. However, knowing his frame of mind, I was able to understand and work effectively with him.

And When the Knife Is in *Your* Back . . . .

It's easy to share stories about overcoming feelings of hate and revenge, but it's another matter when the knife is sticking in *your* back. Then "turning the other shoulder blade" is a painful reality, not a tidy theory.

When it happened to me I was thirty years old and had been with New York Life for five years. I had worked my way up from sales agent to manager of a small office in Wheeling, West Virginia, working with eight agents.

Then came the news that I had been promoted to Toledo office general manager. One gray January day Audrey and I began driving to Toledo to look for a home. I was excited about taking over the larger office. As I would be working with sixteen agents, it was quite a step up.

Halfway to Toledo we stopped for gas and I stepped into a phone booth to let the Toledo general manager know we would arrive the next day. He was slated to take over an even larger office.

As we talked, however, I noted he was not as effusive as he usually had been with me. Finally, he said, "Lee, you'd better give the regional vice-president a call before you get here." He wouldn't add anything and I hung up the phone feeling a sense of disquiet. I quickly dialed our regional vice-president, who seemed to have been expecting my call. When he heard that Audrey and I planned to spend the night in Cleveland before going on to Toledo he said, "Good, you'll be here this evening. Let's have a late dinner together."

When I got back to the car, Audrey looked at my face and asked me what was wrong.

"I don't know," I said, accelerating onto the highway, "but I don't like it." I told her about the call.

We drove on to Cleveland in somber silence. On top of the growing unrest within me, the weather turned bad and soon one of those lake-effect snowstorms engulfed us in a white blur. An hour later our right front tire blew and the car lumbered to a stop. It took me half an hour amid the blinding snow to change it. By the time we reached Cleveland it was ten o'clock. We dragged our suitcases into our room, freshened up as well as we could, and went downstairs. The regional vice-president met us in the dining room which, fortunately, was still open for dinner.

After settling down and giving the waiter our orders, the regional vice-president leaned across the table. "Lee, I have to tell you this and I want to be frank about it."

I stared at him.

"We're creating a new office for you in Akron. It won't be as big as Toledo, but it's a great opportunity."

I was dumbfounded. "But why?"

"Well," he said, straightening his napkin, "there's a problem."

"Problem?"

"Well, remember Tom?"

"Yes." He was a young assistant manager in the Toledo office. We had had breakfast together at an honors meeting and I thought we hit it off rather well.

"Well, he has the idea that you wouldn't be right for the office, that," he folded and refolded his napkin, "you think you're a hotshot and a rah-rah boy."

I leaned forward to speak, but he motioned me back and continued. "He has the ear of an older person in Toledo who is close to the president. The older man called the home office and objected to your coming to Toledo."

I leaned back in my chair, stunned, not believing what I was hearing. Audrey's hand stole into mine and I gripped it.

"Now, it isn't as bad as all that," he hurried on. "Believe me, Lee, we know what a good job you can do and we want you to handle the new Akron office."

The longer he talked, the lower I felt. The Akron office, from his description, was smaller than the one I was leaving in Wheeling.

Anger flooded me. Looking directly at the vice-president, I said, "I'm beginning to think it would be best to leave the company."

His brow furrowed. "Lee, think about Akron. Don't do anything rash."

The rest of the dinner was gloomy. We finished, said our good-nights, and Audrey and I went up to our room, where I let my anger explode.

I paced up and down. I wept. I shook fists and pounded tables. Audrey cried, not because of the job situation but for the way I was acting.

That night I couldn't sleep. At one o'clock in the morning our room phone rang. It was the president of New York Life.

"Lee, we're doing this for your own good," he said. "If we sent you to Toledo, you'd have problems."

I knew he was a caring, compassionate man, so finally, I agreed to try it. Even so, I felt lower than a snake's belly button the next morning when we drove to Akron. We rented a storefront and started operations with eleven agents, most of whom were inexperienced in the field.

Resentment still seethed within me: anger at the man who had stabbed me in the back and anger at those who had listened to him. At that time, I hadn't learned how to tap my power source. I was terribly hurt and didn't know how to handle my feelings.

I did one thing right, however. I translated the anger into a burning determination to do the best possible job I could with the Akron office. I had already learned a good lesson about personal relationships, the most important of which, I felt, was *trust*. Somehow a trust had been violated in the Toledo situation; I saw firsthand how it could hurt people and relationships.

With this in mind, I started out to earn the trust of the men in my office. I visited with them in their homes, was open and honest in working with them. They knew I would do anything to help them. And this was reciprocated when I solicited their help in finding new agents. Something happened in that little Akron office. We created an atmosphere of mutual respect and, yes, you could even use the word *love*. We became a kind of brotherhood where all of us were working together. I know it's a cliché, but we truly lived out the slogan "One for all and all for one."

Within three years, our business had expanded to where we employed fifty-one agents, and Akron was one of the largest offices in the nation.

The president, who had asked me to stay on that night in Cleveland, personally witnessed my receiving the New York Life President's Trophy for the best record in agency building. I was proud to accept it on behalf of the men working with me.

Would it all have happened if I hadn't been "stabbed in the back"? I doubt it. Without the pain and heartache of Toledo, I probably would not have had the incentive to "show them." Fortunately, I was motivated to show them in a positive way and my

Akron staff appreciated it. They never knew about the knife in my back, but they were more than ready to respond to a manager who demonstrated fairness and concern for them as people. I guess you could say there are times when a "good stab in the back" can even be healthy in the long run!

Next time you are stabbed in the back—and it will happen if you are out there in the business world—think about the examples in these chapters. There are many ways that you can "turn the other shoulder blade." There will be times when you will be placed in a situation where you will be forced to develop and learn valuable lessons. Perhaps there is no more difficult principle to learn than refusing to lash out or strike back when you know you've been grossly wronged. But if you can learn that secret, there is no more powerful force you can put to work to make life better for yourself and those around you.

Summing Up

The Principle of Turning the Other Shoulder Blade

When you are stabbed in the back:

1. Remember that revenge is never sweet, always bitter.

2. Don't take the time to strike back, only to reach out and help.

3. Grudges do not flourish in an atmosphere of open communication.

4. For every action there is an opposite and equal reaction.

5. Biting your tongue is almost always better than biting off heads.

6. Checking out a rumor is better than passing (or believing) one.

7. A "knife in the back" can be a blessing in disguise.

3
The Principle of
Mea Culpa

Our country's thirty-third president, Harry Truman, is remembered for several things. Almost everyone knows about the famous sign on his desk that proclaimed: THE BUCK STOPS HERE. Most people cite this cryptic message to prove that Harry Truman was a tough CEO, but I think it was his way of letting people know that, come what may, he was ready to give up his pride and his ego in accepting responsibility when something went wrong. And the nation respected him for it.

Of course, he made mistakes. But when he did, he stood behind them.

Contrast this with a later president who refused to admit he was wrong when everything pointed to it. Beleaguered by the press, he continued to sidestep the blame, which only intensified attack and, in the end, forced him to resign.

An intelligent man who had contributed much in his presidency, he and the nation both suffered tragically.

What would have happened if this same president had stepped forward at the beginning of the situation and accepted blame? I believe it all would have quieted down and been forgotten within a few months.

Accepting blame for a mistake defuses the antagonism the error may engender. By the same token an attempt to duck rightful blame draws scorn.

We All Need a Latin Lesson

There is a Latin phrase, *mea culpa,* which many executives I know have put to good use. It means "I am the culprit; I am to blame." Simply put, mea culpa means that when a person makes a mistake he immediately goes to the person it most affects and admits blame. The sooner he does it the better. Mea culpa can disarm a potentially volatile situation, clear the air, and keep everyone on a positive footing.

The trouble is, admitting blame is not exactly a favorite pastime of most people. Ducking the blame, pointing a finger at someone else, is one of the most crippling weaknesses in our society. A vital shipment is delayed, a valuable customer lost, an accounting mistake costs a firm thousands of dollars. And usually the one responsible spends more time and effort proving he wasn't to blame than he could have spent rectifying the error.

Mea culpa can be especially effective in a situation where no one knows exactly where the blame really lies, but it usually takes a strong leader to handle it. The old country saying goes: "Don't blame you, don't blame me, blame that guy behind the tree."

The origin of *scapegoat* is fascinating—and instructive. In Old Testament times the Israelite priests would bring two goats to the Temple on a special "Day of Atonement." One goat would be sacrificed for the sins of the people, but just to make sure all sins were accounted for, the priests declared the other animal a "scapegoat," which was driven into the wilderness to bear away all sins of the nation for that year. The goat—a perfectly innocent party—was made to pay the price for the entire group.

Does all that sound rather familiar? Today—especially in business—everyone seems to always be looking for a scapegoat.

Back when television first began to be such a success, executives of a major firm thought it would be the perfect medium for training its many salesmen. Films of sales techniques would be made at headquarters and distributed to the firm's many offices nationwide.

Enthusiastic about the idea, corporate leaders brought an agency manager in from the field and put him in charge of the television training program. The man knew all about salesmanship. Unfortunately, he knew little about television techniques.

After the firm had spent half a million dollars to install a studio and buy equipment, they suddenly realized that a terrible mistake had been made. Not only did the project's exorbitant expense far outweigh its benefits but the television system was not proving practical.

Did the executives admit they had erred in not carefully analyzing the program beforehand from both cost and effect standpoints? Did they admit they had put a man completely unversed in the complicated field of television in charge of the project?

No. They fired the man. They found a scapegoat, someone on whom they could lay their sins and send out into the wilderness. It all had a dismal effect within the organization.

What should have been done? The corporate leader, the one in charge of the entire operation, could have employed the principle of mea culpa (I am to blame). He could have called in the executives involved with the project and said, "Gentlemen, it's clear that we have made a mistake. And I'll take full responsibility."

By employing the principle of mea culpa, the one in charge could have led his team in a corrective measure that would have expiated the guilt for everyone while placing himself in a better position to lead the team in corrective measures. As a result, his personal prestige would have risen higher, and morale would have risen throughout the organization.

Men and women instinctively like and trust the person who is willing to accept responsibility when things go wrong, who is willing to take the blame. There is something fresh and inspiring about such an individual.

Of course, mea culpa isn't just for the main leaders in an organization. When an employee makes a mistake, mea culpa can save a serious situation from becoming a disaster. The natural reaction from an employee is fear and the temptation to waffle or weasel out of a situation, but this usually makes the problem worse and eventually the mistake is discovered anyway. If the employee has the courage to use mea culpa quickly, it can save the day and perhaps his job.

I know a young man who was involved in preparing shipments of merchandise in a factory. One afternoon while glancing over bills of lading, he suddenly saw to his dismay that he had routed a vital shipment to the wrong customer. He sat transfixed for a moment, realizing that this could well cost him his job. He also saw that if he kept quiet about it there was a possibility the error might not be traced back to him.

Yet he knew he could not let the mistake slide. Summoning his courage, he stepped into his supervisor's office and explained what had happened. For a moment the supervisor looked startled, but then quickly began an attempt to rectify the mistake. After checking the shipping orders, he got on the phone, reached the trucking company, and was able to have the shipment rerouted.

"Mike," he said to my young friend, "you made a mistake, yes. But your having the courage to come in here and tell me about it right away made it possible for us to correct it." He shook the younger man's hand and added, "I like your kind of attitude."

When You Stumble

"What separates the winners from also-rans is how they bounce back," reports Walter Kiechel III in his article "When a Manager Stumbles," which appeared in *Fortune* magazine. "In reflecting on their own histories, even high achievers admit major stumbles," writes Kiechel, who reveals the result of interviews with eighty-six successful FORTUNE 500 executives by researchers from the Center for Creative Leadership, a nonprofit group in Greensboro, North Carolina.

Sixty-six percent of the executives reported either missing promotions, being exiled to poor jobs, being caught in a major conflict with the boss, contributing to a business failure, or simply being overwhelmed by the enormousness of the job.

In another center study, researchers compared the careers of 20 successful executives with those of 20 so-called derailed executives from the same companies. Both types had made mistakes. But where the also-rans typically tried to deny or conceal their errors, or blame them on others, the managerial winners stepped up to them—forewarning colleagues, trying to solve the problems caused, and then, when the dust had settled and the lessons had been learned, moving on to think about something else.[1]

In other words, the successful managers acknowledged their mistakes. They used them as an opportunity for self-examination, learned what they could from them, were open about them to their colleagues, and usually discovered that the payoff was more enduring than the crisis.

The Day Bill Lear Grounded Himself

Sometimes the fate of an entire enterprise can hang on the right person's admitting responsibility. It happened in 1966 when a well-known inventor faced an agonizing dilemma: risk losing the work of a lifetime, or take the chance that people might die.

Bill Lear, one of the most prolific inventors of our time, faced his decision of mea culpa shortly after the first of his famous Learjet airplanes took to the air. A new concept in private aircraft, the Learjet is an eight-seat, 560 mph aircraft offering the business world fast and economical executive travel. It was a revolutionary new design. Priced much lower than similar jets, the high-performance craft had received favorable publicity worldwide.

Lear and his wife, Moya, had put their hearts, souls, and fortune into getting the first Learjet off the ground. It had rolled off the assembly line in 1963 and by 1966 there were fifty-five Learjets in the air with orders for fifteen more on their factory's books. It had been a struggle for the Lears—but now everything looked bright for their company.

Then, within one month two Learjets crashed under mysterious circumstances. People had died in each of the crashes, both of which seemed unexplainable. Each accident happened shortly after the plane had taken off. Ground control, watching the plane's blip on radar, reported that it suddenly disappeared. There was no word from the pilot, not even a hint of the trouble which could have caused it. Pilot error seemed to be the only answer. Yet, something deep within Bill Lear couldn't accept that.

When he received news of the second crash, he told his wife, "There is only one thing to do. Ground every Learjet until we can find out what's wrong."

Moya looked at her husband with concern. "You mean announce that openly?"

He nodded.

"But are you sure it's a fault in the plane?"

"I don't know," he said, "but we have to find out."

"Well," answered Moya, "there's going to be an awful lot of fireworks among the company executives."

She was right.

"You're out of your mind, Bill!" his associates chorused. "Do you want to destroy the company? If you tell the owners to ground their ships you'll lose everyone's confidence. We're under no obligation to do that; there is absolutely no evidence it's a design or structural flaw.

"Of course," they continued, "we can quietly launch our own crash program to investigate the situation. But we're under no legal obligation to make a public announcement of it. Please, Bill," they pleaded, "think it over!"

Bill Lear did think it over. He went out into his firm's hangar one night and sat in the cockpit of his own Learjet. As he stared out the sleek, swept-back windshield, he meditated on everything that had led up to the creation of this plane. Then his thoughts flitted back to his boyhood, to the hours he had spent poring over his Tom Swift and Horatio Alger books, learning about boys who invented the impossible and accomplished the unbelievable.

He also remembered the countless Sundays he had spent in church listening to his pastor talk about courage and honesty and what God expects of His people. Bill Lear never had the chance to finish high school, but through his church he had learned the basics of living.

As he sat in that dark, quiet jet, he faced his decision. From a business standpoint he knew his associates were right. It certainly wasn't good for the company to publicly admit something might be wrong with its plane, or for him to take the blame for something he might not have to. Despite the mysterious crashes, he and his associates were convinced the Learjet was the finest aircraft of its kind in the world.

As he sat alone there in the plane through the night, he thought of the years of struggle it had taken to achieve this new concept in aircraft. Experts had tried to tell him that his ideas were too advanced, that such dreams could not become realities. He smiled to himself, remembering how he had pointed to the Royal Air Force's fifty-page treatise on why the jet engine would never replace the propeller.

Yes, developing the Learjet had been a struggle. Now, everything could go down the drain if he went ahead with his announcement. But then, Bill weighed the alternative. What if another one went down? What if more lives were lost? Could he live with himself? Was anything worth that?

He rose from the pilot's seat and stepped out of the plane. He knew then that there was only one thing to do. The next day, acting on Bill Lear's orders, the firm contacted all Learjet owners and advised them to ground their planes until the company completed an investigation.

Immediately, the press picked up the news and, of course, it caused a stir throughout the business world. Some of the firms who had ordered Learjets canceled their contracts.

But Bill Lear didn't worry about that. He was driven by something far more important. There *was* an answer; he had to believe that. Fired by his expectation, he set to work, trying to figure out just what had happened.

He began by taking his own jet apart piece by piece, studying each part for a clue. He found nothing amiss. Then, he remembered his boyhood fascination with A. Conan Doyle's books about Sherlock Holmes. He decided to employ the great detective's famous principle of unraveling a mystery by looking for common denominators. What common factors were involved in both crashes? He soon found out. Both planes had taken off in a

warm rain, climbed fast to twenty-four thousand feet, then leveled. Suddenly, as their speed increased, they disappeared from
the radar screen. It all seemed to relate to rain, altitude, and
speed.

As Bill Lear considered this, he was drawn to study the plane's
elevators, that movable part of the tail wing that makes a plane
climb or dive. He studied them, noting their drain holes to let out
the rainwater that collects in these hollow wing assemblies.

Could those drain holes have something to do with it? He
wondered. He analyzed them in ratio to speed, aerodynamic
pressure, altitude—suddenly, he had a shocking insight.

It was a remote possibility, and one that should never happen.
But as he studied his computations, he saw an ominous pattern
taking shape before him. Normally the rainwater would drain.
But if a plane quickly climbed to twenty-four thousand feet, the
water could freeze in the frigid, rarified atmosphere before it had
a chance to drain out. Then the weight of the trapped frozen
water could change the center of balance of the elevators, causing
them to flutter as the plane increased speed, throwing the ship out
of control.

Bill thought long and hard about this theory. It all could happen only under unusual circumstances, but. . . .

There was only one thing to do, he decided: fly the jet himself
and prearrange the same conditions, fastening two-ounce weights
to the back of each elevator, duplicating the effect of the frozen
water. He buckled himself into the pilot's seat, said a prayer,
and took off. The jet shot into the blue like a bullet. At twenty-
four thousand feet he leveled it off and pushed the throttle
forward.

The air-speed needle swung to 450 mph, 500 mph, 550 mph.
Suddenly, the jet seemed to explode with a vibration that sent
gauges flying from the instrument panel. Bill hung onto the control wheel with all his strength. If he had not prepared himself for
the vibration, the plane would have torn itself from his control
and crashed.

He immediately cut speed and was barely able to level the ship.
As he dropped back down to the airport and landed, he knew he

had the answer to the problem. It involved a simple design change in the elevator drain holes. Teams of company men rushed around the world making corrections on the grounded planes. Within three days all Learjets were flying again.

It was a year before the company fully gained back public confidence in Learjets. But it did come back, perhaps more than it would have if Bill Lear had ducked making his public acknowledgment of responsibility. For again, people are attracted by a man or woman who forthrightly takes the blame for an error and tries to do something about it. Not only did all the companies that had canceled their orders come back to reorder, but the plane zoomed in popularity. Today, about one thousand Learjets are flying safely all over the world.

Bill Lear went on to develop many other new revolutionary concepts in aviation before he died in 1978. He made mistakes during his life; in fact, one could say some of his mistakes cost lives. But when the buck came his way, he didn't pass it. He caught it. He admitted his errors, corrected them, and went on. Obviously, he knew the principle of accepting responsibility, but I believe he knew another secret that can be even more important than saying, "I was wrong."

The Hardest Person to Forgive Is Yourself

Forgiving yourself after admitting your errors is the secret I have in mind. To forgive others is hard enough, but to forgive yourself when you feel you have really made a serious mistake is difficult and sometimes seemingly impossible.

Many persons are less concerned with the difficulties caused by their mistake than they are with the blame they place on themselves. Long after the wrong is rectified, the blame molders in the mind, conscious or subconscious, festering and seeping through all their thoughts. This is especially true when the error is a moral one.

We have no right to judge ourselves in such a foolish way, but we do. And we drag guilt around like a huge ball and chain. If we are truly sorry for our mistake, the way out of guilt's clammy clasp is to admit it, try to make it right, and avoid making that mistake again. Good theory, but for many of us it doesn't work quite that easily. Why? Too many of us labor under the stern eye of a father figure lodged in our subconscious. Many people are kept from any meaningful or helpful faith in God because they confuse this warped and twisted father figure with the Almighty. They think He is in the business of making life miserable for anyone who willfully or even unknowingly blows it.

For years psychiatrists have struggled to get troubled clients to not feel guilty. They have tried to "help" them by explaining away the problem or finding a scapegoat, like a domineering parent or teacher. But for a great many people the guilt remains and gets worse.

An encouraging note was sounded in 1973 when psychiatrist Karl Menninger, founder of the famed Menninger Foundation, wrote a startling book titled *Whatever Became of Sin?* One of the most respected men in his profession, Menninger boldly declared that sin is real, not a myth, and the best way out of guilt is to confess errors or wrongdoing, accept forgiveness from God, others—*and oneself*—and get on with life.[2]

A prime example of how all this can work in the everyday world of business is an insurance agent I will call Bob Brand. He was doing quite well but allowed his love of the good life to affect his judgment. He purchased a much larger home, an expensive sports car, and enrolled his children in costly private schools. To bolster his ego, he hired a larger office staff. Then came the day of reckoning when he discovered he was not making enough money to support his life-style.

He faced two choices. He could admit his problem, let some of his staff go, let his children attend public school, and sell the car. But he couldn't do it. He couldn't give up the image he felt he had to maintain to continue to earn the respect of his fellow townspeople.

The other choice? He saw only one alternative: run the premium payments he collected from his clients through his own personal bank account rather than relay them directly to his firm. He did not believe he was stealing. But in the mingling of funds, he was delaying the premium payments, robbing Peter to pay Paul, so to speak.

Of course this couldn't last long. And the day came when Bob found himself in a terrible bind. This was the day he finally surrendered his pride and his security. For he decided to admit everything to his agency supervisor. He felt that even if he wasn't prosecuted, he would certainly lose his job.

Even so, he went to his supervisor and confessed his guilt. He told him how much he loved the insurance business, that he wanted to remain in it, and placed himself completely at his supervisor's mercy.

Honest repentance is a powerful force. The agency supervisor perceived Bob Brand's sincerity. He accepted his plea for forgiveness. Bob sold his sports car, placed his children in public schools, and gradually worked himself back into a sound financial footing. Most important, he forgave himself for his own greed and stupidity. Today he is an outstanding success in the insurance business.

Oh, Bob Brand didn't get off scot-free. It hurt to admit his errors and change his life-style. But in the end he emerged all the better for it. Interestingly, none of his contemporaries seemed to notice his change of life-style, a fact which I have found is more the norm than not. It seems everyone is too busy with his own affairs to notice whether his neighbor is driving a Mercedes or a Ford.

Is the Other Guy's Mistake Really My Business?

Before leaving the subject of catching—not passing—the buck we should look at one other problem that confronts most of us from time to time. It's one thing to face your own mistakes and admit them, as Bill Lear and Bob Brand did; but what do you do when you see a fellow worker or someone close to you making a serious error or pursuing the wrong course? Do you speak up? Is the buck on your desk or is it better to say, "That's none of my business"?

But what should happen when one employee sees a co-worker

about to make a mistake, especially if it might work out to the first employee's advantage? Should he or she let it happen, figuring this is how one's luck is made?

I can think of a prime example in an incident that happened to a friend who is an editor on a national magazine. My friend was going over galleys of a forthcoming issue when he noticed a glaring error in an article handled by an older editor of higher rank.

Relations between the two had not been good; my friend felt that the older man looked down on him to the point of being patronizing and even sarcastic.

For some time my friend sat at his desk, looking at the error. Being human, his first impulse was to let it ride. "It will serve the old goat right," he told himself. "Maybe it will take him down a notch or two, and maybe some of the rest of us will get noticed around here for a change."

But somehow my friend couldn't allow himself to follow his jungle instinct. He let go of his antipathy and self-interest and let compassion take over.

Rising from his desk, he walked into the older editor's office and quietly pointed out the error, adding, "I'm sure you would have caught it but I thought I should mention it anyway."

The older man grimaced and said nothing, his knuckles whitening as he studied the page proofs. The younger man quietly left the room, unsure as to whether or not he had done the right thing.

Ten minutes later the older editor stepped into his office. For a moment he struggled with the words, then he managed to say, "Er, uh, I just want to thank you for bringing that to my attention. It could have been a nasty one."

That was all he said. But from that day on my friend had an influential ally in the company, someone who was ready to both help and boost him at every opportunity.

What would have happened if my friend had just let the error ride? He could easily have said, "It's really not my affair. He'll probably not be that grateful anyway, and for all I know he'll get defensive and make things tougher on me than ever."

Whether my friend realized it or not, the buck had floated in over his desk and he had the choice of catching it or passing it on.

If he had passed it on, the older man's effectiveness could have been impaired, his confidence shaken, and the entire magazine undermined. Thousands of readers would have jumped on that particular error and many of them wouldn't have forgotten it in a hurry.

Of course, in one way it was easy for my friend to play good guy in the white hat. In this case he received gratitude and approval. But what happens when you move in on a friend who doesn't want your help—someone who is making a mistake in his personal life?

For example, what if you discover that a married friend is having an affair? Today, the world tells us that we are supposed to turn a blind eye to such things. "Don't get involved," is the usual advice. However, if you value your friend, I believe you will get involved by visiting him or her in a quiet place to talk about it.

Let me tell you about two men I know who had such a visit. We'll call them Jim Gibson and Frank Masters. Frank, husband and father of two young boys, was having an affair with a woman in his firm. It was obvious to other employees who gossiped about it during coffee breaks. Jim, who worked in the same department, was a close friend of Frank. It would have been easy for Jim to ignore the situation. After all, in our "enlightened" age such things happen all the time.

Jim, however, had great love and respect for his friend and in good conscience did not feel he could let it pass. He actually prayed long and hard for guidance in facing him. A few days later he made a luncheon date with Frank; they met at a quiet corner table in a restaurant.

"Frank," began Jim, "you know how much I value your friendship. And because of that your situation involves me."

"I know what you mean," said Frank, grimly stirring his coffee. "But I think you're stepping out of your territory, don't you?"

This is the moment most men would have drawn back. But Jim loved and cared for Frank and his family.

"Frank, in a way it is my territory," Jim replied, "because I don't want to go through the pain of seeing you suffer."

The conversation became heated but in the end the two were

finally able to talk openly. It was months before Frank was able to end his liaison, but he and Jim are still close friends. And I believe it all came about because Jim had the courage to face his friend in his friend's best interest.

Jim had to risk his pride in bringing up the affair, and he took a real chance of losing Frank's friendship. He had to take a chance and make himself vulnerable.

Is it worth it? I struggle with my answer to that question, just as you do, but it helps me to remember that anyone can drop the ball. It takes a stronger person to catch the buck. And that strength must come from a higher power.

How does one tap that power? Through instinct, conscience, and prayer.

Summing Up

The Principle of Mea Culpa

When you are responsible in whole or in part for a mistake:

1. Employ the principle of mea culpa. Accepting your share of the blame almost always lessens the pain and penalties the error may have caused.

2. Don't use mea culpa unless you are ready to pay the penalty.

3. Look for the plus in the mistake, but learn from what you have done wrong; make lemonade out of a lemon.

4. Once the mistake is admitted, forgive yourself. You can't be of much help to the company if you're dragging a big bag of guilt behind you.

5. When mistakes are made, try to think of remedies, not recriminations. Good business is problem solving, not finding scapegoats.

6. When you see another person making a mistake, try to help him or her, even if it means you risk being misunderstood. To watch someone make a mistake and not try to help him is one of the subtler forms of passing the buck.

—4—
The Principle of Relinquishing Worry

Does this sound familiar to you?

Early in our marriage, my wife, Audrey, said I was suffering from what she called the "cannibal complex." When I'd come home from work, jaw set, brow furrowed over job problems, and pick at the dinner she had so carefully prepared, she'd sigh, "Lee, you're letting those worries eat you up. You're cannibalizing yourself with anxiety!"

Audrey was right, only I wouldn't admit it then. That's one of the reasons I suffered a massive heart attack in my later years. I was one of that unfortunate legion of people who let problems eat into them until the tension develops a cardiac condition.

My main problem was that I didn't know the difference between *worry* and *concern.*

Recently I looked up these words in *Webster's Dictionary.*

Worry means "uneasy, disturbed, being in a state of pain."

Concern indicates "taking an interest in."

The root derivations of these two words are telling. *Worry* comes from the Anglo-Saxon *wyrgan,* meaning "choke, strangle, injure, violate, pester, and annoy." Its sister word *anxious* comes from the Latin *angere* meaning "to trouble, choke."

On the other hand, the word *concern* stems from the Late Latin *concernere,* meaning "to mix, mingle, as in a sieve." It also comes from the Latin words *con* and *cernere,* "to separate, to sift."

As I see it, being concerned about a problem means sifting or sorting out the best ways to face it.

I believe we were designed to be concerned, but not worried or anxious.

It's difficult to do this, I know. It took me a long time to learn how to relinquish my worries. One of the many times I suffered over this happened some years ago when one of my four daughters, Lisa, was giving me trouble. At least, that's what I called it. She was going with a young man I didn't like. I had reason to believe he was involved with drugs and that my daughter was experimenting with marijuana. I was eaten up with anxiety.

When they went out for an evening, I would lie awake until they returned. One night was especially long. The gray light of dawn had begun to silhouette the maples outside our bedroom window before I heard the car tires on our driveway.

Aflame with anger, I threw on a robe, stormed down the stairs, and confronted Lisa and the boy at the door. After literally throwing the young man out of the house, I sent a tearful Lisa to her room. She was grounded for two months—no dates, entertainment, or social life.

Meanwhile I was consumed with anxiety about what would eventually happen to her. Would she run away and marry the boy? What kind of life would she have? I mentally projected all kinds of disasters.

The church Audrey and I were attending (by this time I was accompanying her to services) had some excellent counselors and Audrey prevailed on me to seek their help.

"I think Lisa needs it more than I do," I glowered.

"Well, take her, too," suggested Audrey.

When I broached the subject to Lisa, she said she would go if her boyfriend could accompany us. I grudgingly gave in.

The counselor was warm and friendly. After listening to all three of us, then speaking separately with Lisa and the boy, he took me aside.

"Lee," he said gently, *"you* are the one with the problem."

"Me?" The good father who only worried about his daughter's well-being?

"Yes, you," he said. "You're bound up in anxiety over the situation."

I stared at him in disbelief. What kind of counseling was this? Obviously, I felt, he was working for the other side.

Lisa left with her boyfriend and I drove home alone, seething.

After slamming the door of our house behind me, I threw my hat on to a chair and answered Audrey's questioning look with, "The kid has won. None of it did any good."

For three days I sulked. Finally, I tried to take the counselor's advice. I relinquished my worry.

Nothing really happened for the next several weeks. Everything seemed to remain the same. Lisa resumed dating the boy and continued to stay out late.

But by this time my attitude was beginning to change. *Believing* that it was going to be taken care of, I felt a sense of peace. Of course, I was concerned. I did not worry but I did continue to pray for Lisa and her friend.

Ultimately, I learned to apply what the counselor taught me in business and other areas of my life.

I was learning the difference between *concern* and *worry.* Certainly, as a loving parent I should have been concerned about Lisa's life-style. But true concern was placing the situation in other hands. There are some things we can't force. My earlier worry was allowing the situation to strangle and pester me in my frustration at not being able to do anything about it.

In time, everything changed. The boy went away to college and Lisa chose a different school. They never dated again. It ended, just like that. Today, some years later, Lisa is happily married to a fine young man.

Sidetracking Stress

The sad part of it all is that when we get anxious we often end up making mistakes. As you can see from the above, I have made my share of mistakes. One of the reasons for this is I am by nature a Type A person, someone very susceptible to stress, who lets his emotions run away with him. To counter this, I try to remember some suggestions made by Dr. Denis Waitley, a national authority on stress management. He outlined them in his book *Seeds of Greatness*. They are commonsense principles that will help anyone, I believe. I've adapted them here for you.

1. Let your sense of humor run free. We all have it but we tend to suppress it, thinking it is only a warehouse for jokes and anecdotes. But watch how children laugh at almost anything—puppies, bugs, merry-go-rounds, and their own faces in a mirror.

   As long as we can look at ourselves and life through the eyes of a child, and not take ourselves too seriously, we have learned the essence of meeting life's changes. And since change is inevitable, we then can know that tomorrow will bring a new surprise, a new challenge, a new delight. And, above all, let humor help you perceive your own occasionally ludicrous aspects.

2. Recognize the fact that you *own your emotions*. Take responsibility for them. When you reprimand someone or express your unhappiness, try to do so after the urge to fight or become upset has subsided (the old count-to-ten theory). Remember, you are usually ineffective when angry. You get your feelings across better in a normal voice, without all the warlike body language. When upset, try a substitute physical exercise to work off the adrenaline, such as jogging or chopping wood. Of course, speak your mind. But criticize the behavior without attacking the person. No one wins an argument. You can only win an agreement.

3. Remember, there is nothing as permanent as change. Try to stay flexible.

4. Steer clear of "all or nothing" management. If things don't work out as planned, then salvage the good of it. I'll always remember being in an hour-long traffic tie-up and, while most of us stewed and fretted in our cars, one family spread a picnic lunch on the green grass beside the highway and enjoyed the hour respite. Recognize that you and others will never be perfect, so make allowances.

5. Let others be responsible for their own behavior. Don't assume blame or guilt for wrongs that others commit. Beyond reasonable respect for law and personal safety, even your children are in charge of their own lives. Of course, help them and others when-

ever you can, but let courage and flexibility be your basic guides.

6. Learn that saying no can be an attribute. One of the best ways to relieve stress is to schedule your time so that you can comfortably keep your commitments. Being "under the gun" all the time increases the risk for coronary and other stress-related diseases (as I can affirm from my own experience). Saying no in advance is much less painful than admitting later on, "I'm sorry I can't deliver." Only *you* can put yourself under the gun.

7. Simplify your life. Get rid of clutter and ask yourself regularly, "Beyond the normal routine of my daily work and schedule, on what do I really want to spend my time?"

8. Enjoy the inspiration of recreation. Get out the kites, grab the Frisbees, dust off the picnic basket, have fun with the children, attend little-theater productions, musicals, and make sure that your television and movie viewing includes shows that warm the heart.[1]

"Sounds great," you may say, "but what about all the difficult decisions we face in our everyday life?" Of course, I realize we can't address with mirth the question "Which house shall we buy?" or "What should we do about Aunt Ida, who can no longer live alone?"

But I do believe we can find guidance. Naturally, we should exhaust every source available to us from friends and relatives who have had experience with the problem to experts in the field involved.

Even so, it finally comes down to making our own decision. That is when we must tap our secret source of power. At times like these, I pray. But before I do this I must be certain that my mind and heart are open. This means relinquishing all negative thoughts of ill will and unforgiveness toward anyone. Otherwise, these feelings tend to clog one's receptiveness.

In prayer I express myself completely: my desires, fears, yes, even guilts. And after asking the question, I *listen*. Don't rattle off a list of wishes, then get up and leave. That's like submitting a grocery list, not praying. God speaks to us in many ways. Solutions and answers have a way of percolating to the surface; some of them will surprise you with their clear logic. Then use the brain with which you have been blessed—this wonderful instrument of analysis and deduction which no man-made computer will ever equal. And take action. Once you determine in your heart what is right, then step out in faith and *do* it.

A Cottage by the Sea?

Friends have told me how they have found answers. One man's most difficult decision was resolved with an answer that would not ordinarily sound practical. Yet, as it worked out, it had the wisdom of Solomon.

Henry Jackson, a publication editor, lived in New Jersey at the time. I knew him and his family quite well. For a number of years Henry, his wife, and two young sons had loved vacationing in a lovely seaside town on the tip of Cape Ann, Massachusetts, about an hour north of Boston. Each summer they would rent a small cottage for two or three weeks. Of course, after a few years of this, they dreamed of buying a small place in the area. They watched the ads and talked to realtors, but nothing remotely near their pocketbook was available in this costly resort area.

One November in the early seventies, the family spent a weekend on Cape Ann. While walking around town on Saturday morning, Henry found a small real estate office open and stepped inside. Of course, there wasn't anything in his price range on the listings—until the realtor thoughtfully brought a piece of paper out of his desk drawer. "Here's something you might want to look at."

Henry stared at the paper, his hands shaking. The property was almost an acre right on the ocean, a few miles outside of town. On that piece of land sat a house trailer that had been converted into a permanent cottage just large enough to accommodate four people. It would be perfect for their family. He was further shocked when he heard the price the realtor quoted. A ten thousand dollar bid, he thought, would get it. An older widow then living in Boston had no use for the property anymore and wanted to be rid of it. "But you will have to get a firm bid to me by Monday morning," the realtor said, adding, "a buy like this won't be around long."

With thumping heart, Henry Jackson hurried out to see the

property with his family. Even on a gray, winter day it looked good. Breakers curled onto the rock-lined shore and the little trailer-house had a full view of the ocean. Normally, a vacant oceanside acre in this area would sell for ten to fifteen times more than this asking price, but this was one of those rare flukes one runs into in a lifetime.

Henry called the realtor and told him he'd let him know soon—by Monday morning, in fact. During the drive back to New Jersey Henry and his wife excitedly discussed the opportunity. Though they were not very well off financially at the time, they felt they could come up with the price by selling some securities and borrowing the rest.

However, as they talked, a small detail nagged at Hank. He noticed his wife was not as enthusiastic about the property as he was.

"It's fine, Hank," she said, when he questioned her. "Maybe I don't see all the possibilities in it that you do, but I agree it's a real buy. It could be what we've been wanting, but," she turned and put her hand on his arm, "*you* decide. I'll leave it up to you."

Still enthused, Henry went to bed that night planning to write a letter enclosing his bid the next morning.

However, the next day he found himself thinking twice about it. Was it assembling the finances that bothered him? he wondered. No, finances could be arranged. Even though he was hesitant, he was still basically excited about the idea.

By evening, Henry was in a quandary, angry at himself for not being able to make up his mind. His wife assured him of her support. But why wasn't he completely sure about the purchase? When he went to bed that night he was certain of one thing: his bid would have to be wired to the realtor in the morning if he was going to go through with it.

Now Henry was a religious man and he prayed for guidance. He surrendered the whole situation, asking, "Please give me some word by morning." He soon slipped off into sleep, feeling a sense of peace. Sometime later, something awakened him—a dream or a vision—whatever it was had burned these words into his mind: *Why tie yourself down?*

Deep within himself he *knew* this was his answer. With a sense of relief, he phoned the realtor and told him he was not interested in the property.

Today, Henry Jackson will tell you that it was a wise decision.

Friends still hoot at him about it. "Wise? How foolish? You could have turned around and sold that property for twice what you paid! Even better, you could have kept it for ten years and made one hundred thousand dollars on it!"

Henry Jackson smiles and looks at it differently. "For someone else, they could be very right," he says. "But for us, the words I was given that morning had nothing to do with making money. They had everything to do with our quality of life.

"If we had bought that place," he continued, "we would have felt obligated to return there every vacation time, perhaps extra weekends as well. In a very real sense, we would have been tied down.

"Look at what has happened to us since," he pointed out. "We have returned to Cape Ann almost every summer since and have found wonderful places to rent, costing us less in the long run than the taxes and upkeep on that property would have been.

"Moreover, we have enjoyed different localities, different views of the ocean—and our rented houses were much larger and more luxurious than that cottage, making each visit new and fresh and allowing our children to invite their friends to join them. And besides that, one summer our family toured Europe, another time we visited Bermuda. We would never have made those trips if we had owned a summer place."

"But what about the profit you could have realized, Hank?" I pursued, knowing the high price seaside property brings these days.

"Here's how my wife and I look at it," he answered. "Sure, we could have made a lot of money on the deal. But I asked for guidance and I received it. If I'd gone ahead and bought it, that would not have been obedient, and I doubt if things would have turned out as well as they did.

"Besides," he added, "the fun we've had in other places is worth far more than any profit we could have made. And Lee," he added, smiling, "I think God will make up for it in His own way."

As Henry pointed out, buying the property could very well have been the right decision for someone else. In fact, someone did buy it, tore down the trailer cottage, built a new house, and is very happy there.

The point is that if Henry Jackson had not relinquished his anxiety, he would have stewed over his decision ever after, wondering if he had made the wise choice.

Fretting over decisions, past or present, eats into us. As one wise doctor said, "Ulcers do not result from what we eat, but from what eats us." By the same token we can turn the tables on worry by making it a benefit.

The Flat Tire That Launched a Journey

Here's an example. Back in 1934, a young man in New York City by the name of Tom Carvel had just about given up hope of making a career for himself. He had tried everything he could think of—from selling appliances and playing semipro football to playing drums in a jazz combo. Nothing seemed to work out right.

Finally, he built a small trailer which he planned to haul out into the country with his old Model-A Ford sedan. From it, he would sell ice cream, hot dogs, and cold drinks to visitors in a county park.

When the trailer was completed and stocked with refreshments, Tom started out one hot summer morning to the park. However, he had no sooner reached the country road when one of his trailer tires blew out. His heart sank. Miles from his destination, he was trapped on a lonely highway. He had no spare, no tools, and no money to pay for having the tire fixed. To make matters worse, he knew that the ice cream would soon melt. Everything he had invested would soon be lost.

Helpless and hopeless, he slumped down on his car's running board, head in his hands. As with all of us in similar situations, Tom had a choice. He could have sat there consuming himself with worry, anger, and frustration—berating fate, the man who sold him the tire, and eventually abandoning the trailer and driving back to the city in defeat.

Instead, Tom knew something about tapping his power source. Leaning forward, he sighed, "I dream of running my own business someday. But I can't go anywhere with that tire. What am I supposed to do?"

He felt a sense of peace after finishing that simple prayer. Of course the tire did not magically inflate. Nor did a tow truck suddenly appear. However, in a relatively peaceful though concerned state of mind, Tom relaxed against the side of his car and gazed across the road. He noticed a small pottery shop there that appeared to be open. He walked over to it and met the proprietor, who turned out to be a kindly older man.

The two began talking and an idea evolved. Why not bring Tom's trailer over to the pottery shop's parking area and hook it up to the electricity available there? Tom could sell his ice cream to passersby and also help the older man sell his pottery.

The two of them set up the trailer and Tom opened for business. He did so well that he stayed there, discovering the benefit of selling from a stationary location where customers came to know him. His benefactor's pottery business also increased as more cars drove into the parking area.

In his spare time, Tom worked on a mechanical ice cream dispenser and eventually patented his invention. A few years later, he began to sell his homemade ice cream from his own store and that pottery shop became the site of his firm's first ice cream plant.

Today, there are some nine hundred Carvel ice cream shops throughout the United States and many parts of the world. They came about because instead of angrily fretting over his misfortune, Tom Carvel surrendered to a power greater than himself, and that turned a flat tire into the foundation of a thriving business.

Again, we see the Butterfly Effect (which I described at the beginning of this book). When you surrender your worry or your problem to a higher power, you may never be aware of all the ramifications involved, but you can be certain that the end result will be positive.

Straight From the Heart

One day I heard someone emphasize the Bible verse "Let not your heart be troubled."[2] He said that these words tell us about the tragic effects of worry on our personal beings. Anxiety causes stress, one of the major causes of cardiovascular problems.

As I have mentioned before, the classic Type A individual, the hard driver, the person eager to "get it done," whose blood vessels are constricted by stress, is the one whose obituary appears when he is only forty or fifty years old.

In truth, the person who overcomes his impatience and anxiety and works in peace is usually more effective in the long run.

Unfortunately, the world tries to teach us otherwise. Since childhood, we have been exposed through books, movies, and television to the stereotype of the aggressive, pushing person's winning the prize.

In my own business experience, I have seen the fallacy of this image. I knew an officer in one of the world's largest corporations who chose to follow this bitter path. Always hungry for more responsibility, he trod roughshod over many people. He snatched jobs that others should have had and offended many associates. Finally, he reached the point where he was next in line for a top echelon position. But when the appointment was announced, he was passed over.

The person chosen was a quiet individual, almost introverted. However, he did his work calmly, efficiently, with a sense of peace. He was a servant to others and management felt comfortable with him.

It pained me to see the hurt in the first man's eyes, his attempt to pass off his disappointment as "not important," but obviously questioning himself, "What's the use? I struggled so hard and so long and someone else got the job." This man eventually ended up with serious health problems.

Too many of us in the business world take on more responsibility than we should. The more people we supervise, the larger the amount of money passing through our hands, the greater our empire: These are too often the criteria by which we measure our importance.

There will always come the day when some of it is taken away. Then we feel hurt and rejected. Our "security" has been shaken.

After thirty-four years of struggling up the corporate ladder, I have learned that there is absolutely no security in the material world. The only real security lies in your source of power.

Of course, we will face problems no matter what our job. Whether we are a corporate executive, housewife, schoolteacher, or secretary, we will find ourselves under pressure from time to time.

Here are some easy-to-use techniques which can help us effectively meet pressure situations. Top athletes use them in clutch situations, say nationally recognized management consultants Robert and Marilyn Kriegel, who recommend them:

1. Think hard about something which you've handled successfully in the past. The confidence gained from your past experience will steady you in the new one. For example, if you are a salesman, greeting a new prospect isn't much different from meeting someone new at a party.

2. Ask yourself, "What's the worst thing that can happen?" Viewing this realistically lets you see that the result of failure isn't as tragic as you may anticipate.

3. Concentrate on what you can control; avoid worrying about what cannot be handled. For example, if bad weather delays your plane arrival, don't fret over it but think about what steps you can take to remedy the situation when you get to the airport.

4. Imagine yourself in control. Positive imaging, a technique in which you "see" yourself acting calm and cool in a rough situation, is another way of putting into action the Bible verse "As a man thinketh, so is he."[3]

5. Take time each day for relaxation. This could mean a leisurely stroll, settling down with a good book, puttering with a hobby. It doesn't matter what activity you choose, as long as it relaxes you, and you make it part of your daily schedule.

One final word about afflicting pressures: No matter what, they'll always badger us—in our jobs, at home, even when we try to relax. That's life. Try not to take pressures too seriously. They'll be around long after we're gone. They can even be beneficial if we look at them in a positive way.

Remember the dandelion? We all know it as that stubborn weed that flourishes amid all kinds of punishment we gardeners throw at it, from using weed killers to ruthlessly rooting it out.

However, I read about a farmer, Adrian Wells, up in Maine who actually grows them commercially to satisfy gourmets who eat them fresh in salads or cooked. Farmer Wells' problem is that when he puts dandelions in a field with air, sunlight, water, and fertilizer and gently cultivates them, they run into trouble, developing all kinds of problems.

But in his big lawn plus flower and vegetable gardens it's a different story. When the dandelions face the constant pressures of being harassed by weed killers, shouldered aside by bigger, stronger plants, and search for a place in the sun, they thrive beautifully, just as they do in your own lawn.

Maybe we can learn a lesson from the dandelion in that we, too, can flourish in adversity.

Summing Up

The Principle of Relinquishing Worry

1. Sift out worry and concern from the problem. Discard debilitating worry and utilize creative concern.

2. Let your sense of humor take the edge off knifelike worries.

3. Remember that it's how you *react* to a situation, not what it does to you, that determines the outcome.

4. Don't expect perfection in anything. Avoid assuming responsibility for the behavior of others.

5. Learn when to say no. Schedule your time so you can comfortably keep commitments and avoid putting yourself under the gun.

6. Simplify. Simplify. *Simplify.* Leave room in your life for rest and recreation for yourself and others.

5

The Principle of Loyalty

I'm sure you know someone like John Harpling. I last saw him at a wedding reception. As usual, I could just about predict his mood. The band had begun playing when I saw him standing alone near the punch bowl with that distant look of disapproval some people wear at wedding receptions. Whether it's because they feel the bride's parents have spent too much money on the fete or they have just discovered the punch is nonalcoholic, I have never known.

But in John's case I felt fairly sure of what was wrong. I stepped over to him to say hello.

"Oh," he said, looking up over his punch glass at me, "it's the insurance mogul."

Ignoring the remark, I smiled and patted him on the back, since it was obvious he wasn't going to relinquish his punch glass to shake hands.

"How's it going, John?" I asked.

He drained his cup and shook his head.

He didn't have to say anything. I could tell. His job was souring. He had held it for nine months, and from past experience I knew that was about the gestation period for John's disgruntlement.

In another year or so he would be with another firm. And the same thing would take place. In the years I have known John, he has held a number of jobs with various firms. According to John, he has had the misfortune of picking companies all suffering from the same problem: poor management.

At first I sympathized with him when he told me how stupid his superiors were, how they wouldn't listen to him, and how the company had no future because of it. After a while I began to wonder. I noticed that the firms he had left seemed to continue to prosper with no major management changes.

And yet, I believe we all can understand John's feelings, though we usually don't go as far as changing jobs when we get miffed. There have been many times when I have winced at not being able to do things my way. It is only human to believe we know more than the other person. Our basic pride and ego will not let us do otherwise.

This is borne out by a major opinion survey in which motorists were asked to check off their driving skills as "below average," "average," or "above average." Practically everyone marked "above average." How can the majority be above average? Yet, if you are in the passenger seat when I am driving and hear my muttered comments about other motorists, you will note that I hold the same opinion. Somehow our base natures, the "old man" within us, seems to take over most when we are behind the wheel of our car.

The Chromium-Plated Ego

When we accidentally brush each other as we pass on the sidewalk we murmur an apology. But let another motorist cut in front of us when we are driving, and watch out for the Mount Vesuvius eruption of anger and shaking fists.

An explanation for this may be found in some psychologists' opinions that the car we drive is an extension of our ego.

Thus, if another driver cuts us off, our ego suffers and we are offended. And that is where the danger arises—in being offended.

According to *Webster's Dictionary,* when we feel offended, we feel attacked, insulted, and angry. Our feelings are hurt.

Most of the tragedies of history stemmed from someone, or a group of people, feeling offended. Motorists have been known to clamber out of their cars and fight after being offended, sometimes to the point of killing. It is natural to feel offended by another driver's wrongdoing. But the big difference is how we handle it. We have two choices: nurse our anger and strike back or try to understand the other person's situation.

Whether we admit it to ourselves or not, it is easy to feel offended by our boss, our superior, our department head. This is especially true when we feel we know more about the job than he does or when he won't take our suggestions.

The Quiet Struggle

A close friend who felt this way made an interesting discovery. Fred Glantzberg has been a buyer with the Union Carbide Corporation for fifteen years. The son of an air force pilot whose family lived in various parts of the world, Fred grew up as a no-nonsense, highly resourceful individual. After gaining his degree in industrial engineering at Georgia Tech, he joined Union Carbide in 1957 in one of its plant engineering groups, and through the years advanced to his position as senior buyer.

However, in his early years there, Fred found himself chafing under supervision. "Being a company man, I never criticized my boss openly," he said, "but there were many times when I felt I knew more about the job than he did." And so, as happens in many firms and organizations, an undercurrent of struggle existed between Fred and his supervisor. It is at this point where any organization is weakest. This quiet, unspoken warfare becomes a stumbling block to optimum efficiency. It destroys healthy relationships between people. It becomes a fertile field for insidious company politics that can hurt an organization.

In Fred's case something different happened. It started when he began attending a noontime Bible study group at Union Carbide's headquarters in New York City. This led to a growing interest in godly principles. As an engineer, Fred was skeptical. But where his engineering manuals provided technical help in his profession, he began to find in the Bible illuminating guidance for living.

Fred remembers the day when it all came together for him: "I had never felt such freedom before," he said. "It was as if the old Fred Glantzberg, with all his hang-ups, had worn out and a new man was engineered.

"It was while reading the Apostle Paul's letters that the truth about employee-employer relationships really hit me," says Fred. " 'Servants, be obedient to them that are your masters according to the flesh, with fear and trembling, in singleness of your heart, as unto Christ; Not with eyeservice, as menpleasers; but as the servants of Christ, doing the will of God from the heart; With good will doing service, as to the Lord, and not to men: Knowing that whatsoever good thing any man doeth, the same shall he receive of the Lord, whether he be bond or free.'[1]

"That really set me back on my heels," said Fred. "Here, God was telling me to obey my boss not just outwardly but inwardly as well, without chafing and resentment. God was also telling me that I should do my work as if I were doing it directly for Him.

"After reading those words I sat there for a long time, realizing where I had gone wrong. I also came to a decision. From then on, I'd work the way God wanted me to work."

Fred also knew that God did not want him to be a Milquetoast, shrinking back and letting errors happen. "Being intelligent, well informed, and getting your ideas across in a clear, forthright manner is definitely not un-Christian," he says.

The day came when Fred sat down with his boss and told him that although he felt obligated to give him his opinion on situations as they arose, once the boss made his decision, Fred would support him in it all the way.

His supervisor seemed pleasantly surprised. But something far more important happened: As Fred's chafing and "I know better" resentment disappeared, "something clicked," as he put it, in the department. A new bond of trust was forged between the two men. From then on their working relationship prospered. There was a new warmth and a feeling of mutual support, and Fred found himself enjoying his work as he never had before.

A Matter of Choice

In the new openness, Fred felt more free than ever to contribute his ideas. If he saw a problem arising in a decision his boss had made, rather than argue about it, Fred sought an alternative solution which he could present, giving him a choice.

"I got the idea from an old Jewish management book a friend gave me," says Fred. "I had heard of it," he said, "but I had once considered it a collection of legends and fables. However, my friend showed me that it was full of management techniques and problem-solving ideas that had been tested again and again for thousands of years.

" 'Human nature doesn't change,' my friend said. 'What worked then works now.'

"The name of the book?" Fred chuckled. "It's called the Old Testament. And before you turn me off, listen to how one young corporate team leader came up with an alternative solution that worked. He was a young guy by the name of Daniel whose group consisted of three assistants named Shadrach, Meshach, and Abednego. These were names," smiled Fred, "I once thought were only in an old spiritual.

"It all began when Daniel and his group were assigned to a training program in the corporate community of the Babylonian King Nebuchadnezzar. It would be a three-year program from which they were expected to emerge as top advisers to the king.

"The training administrator ordered all young men in the program to take their meals from the executive kitchens, which were renowned for their gourmet food and excellent wines. This is where Daniel and his group found themselves between a rock and a hard place. Being Hebrew, they knew it was against God's wishes for them to eat such food. So Daniel asked his supervisor to let them subsist on only vegetables and water. The supervisor blanched. 'Why you fellows will become pale and thin compared to the rest of the trainees; the CEO will have my head!'

"And this is where Daniel came up with an alternative solution. 'Look,' he said, 'put us on a ten-day diet of only vegetables and water. Then judge how we look at the end of the ten days and *you* decide whether or not we can continue our own diet.'

"The supervisor happily agreed and at the end of the test period Daniel and his three companions looked healthier than the rest of the group who had eaten the king's rich food. From then on, they were allowed to live on their kosher diet.

"By the end of the three years the foursome had developed so well that they became top advisers to the king who, as the Bible says, 'found them ten times better than all the magicians and astrologers that were in all his realm.' "[2] Because he found a suitable alternative, Daniel was able to keep his faith, yet remain loyal to his CEO.

Fred found himself applying the alternative principle in a knotty department problem concerning travel. Purchasing agents must travel to check out the manufacturing methods of the products they buy. But in a time of a lagging economy, Fred's firm had to cut his department's travel budget.

The old Fred would have complained bitterly. However, utilizing the "Daniel factor," he worked out an alternative plan in which one trip would cover two different projects and thus keep travel costs within budget.

He presented the idea to his department head as an alternative. Management liked the idea, Fred was congratulated, and everybody came out ahead.

"Nothing really changes," observes Fred. "A factor that worked well in Daniel's time is just as effective today. As the Bible says, 'There is nothing new under the sun.' " [3]

The Insecurity of Being Right

Of course, there are things besides pride and ego that make an employee resent the one he works under. A thirty-year-old man, whom I will call David Hargrave, came to me for counseling. At first I wondered why this good-looking young man with a master's degree in accounting was seeking help.

I soon found out. In the past five years he had held eight jobs and had been fired from each one. After some conversation with David it was easy to understand why. Not only was he arrogant with an "I can do it all" attitude, but he maintained that he was fired from his previous jobs because he was a "threat to the boss."

"Every time I came up with a good idea, management either negated it or took it over as its own. I guess," he sighed, "it doesn't pay to be too good at your job."

We sat down together in my tennis house, a little secluded shelter set back in the trees in my yard—a setting where it was easy to be open with each other. For three consecutive afternoons we talked openly and frankly about David's situation. After the third afternoon it became clear. David Hargrave was deeply insecure. Thus he tried to compensate by being "right" all the time. He resented criticism and sought applause. This ruled all of his relationships, with his underlying antagonism rankling others and crippling his career.

It took a lot of talking to help David see that there was One he could trust. Finding this, he began to find himself. Freed of his old hang-ups and with his old self out of the way, he was able to objectively view business relationships and see where he fit into the scheme of things.

Finally, working as a team member, he began carving a niche for himself in the business world.

Again, as with Fred Glantzberg, it is right, even vital, for the good of our firm or organization to question management openly and without rancor. But when management makes its decision, we must be loyal in obedience.

Of course, if we feel it is wrong to the point of being dishonest or immoral and management does not accept our alternative offering, then we must follow our guidance and resign, giving management our reasons. There is a point of being obedient to a fault, such as the people who blindly followed Adolph Hitler in his mad course to destruction.

But in the normal course of events, when we are part of an enterprise that is filling a need, whether we are selling cars, insurance, operating a punch press, or programming a computer, when we willingly follow direction with an open heart, we will find the grace and strength to be successful.

Summing Up

The Principle of Loyalty

1. When you find yourself resenting authority, the problem is probably within you.

2. Swelling with self-importance makes you a bigger target for error.

3. Work goes smoother without the grit of chafing or resentment.

4. Remove self from the eyepiece and you'll get an undistorted view of the overall picture.

5. Take off the blinders of misconceptions to see successful alternate routes.

6. When you banish your ego, you send most of your troubles with it.

6

The Principle of Hanging in There

Riding the New Haven commuter railroad into New York City from my home in Connecticut provides some fascinating insights into human nature.

Last fall I shared a seat with a young man from my area who had recently graduated from college; I asked him how his job was progressing.

"Oh," he sighed, leaning back in his seat, "I'm giving it six months and then I'll try something else."

I looked at him sharply. "You mean quit?" I was surprised, for I knew that only six months ago he had joined a firm that was doing quite well.

"Sure," he replied. "A turtle doesn't get anywhere unless he sticks his neck out."

And a rolling stone gathers no moss, I thought to myself.

Of course, I realized my fellow passenger and I were of different generations. He was in his early twenties, I was in my late fifties. I knew there had been a lot of changes in thinking during the intervening thirty years. The young man was more the rule than the exception in his age group. "On the move" seems to be the prevailing mood today. Pick up and start again. And in this competitive world, another job can be a stepping-stone on the way up for an ambitious person.

Yet, as I glanced at the young man who was now quietly looking out the window, I hoped he was reconsidering.

There is much to be said for changing jobs when the move is advantageous. I realize that many in my generation were too conservative in this respect. But after almost half a century in the work force, I believe the right answer lies somewhere in between.

Changing jobs can be a quicker way to advance one's salary, and it can lead to a more fulfilling position. On the other hand, there is much to be said for old-fashioned hanging in there.

I thought back on the resumés of various job applicants I had screened over the past years. If someone had changed jobs too often, seemingly without giving any one of them a chance, I would become a bit suspicious. Why so many moves? Was he or she a malcontent....never satisfied....was he encouraged to leave by former employers?

The bottom-line question I would have to ask myself, as do most hiring executives today, was: "If we put this person through our training program, will the investment pay off? Or, will he stay with us only a year or two and move on?"

Thus, if it was a choice between John Smith, who had held several jobs in the past few years, and Bill Nelson, who had fewer positions but held them longer—with every other consideration equal, Bill Nelson would get my nod.

Every rule has its exception, of course. And when one is thinking of changing employment, there are elements far more important than job longevity to consider.

I like to compare these to the instrument check airline pilots must make before they take their ships onto the runway for takeoff. Oil pressure, ailerons, rudder, radio direction finder.

Changing jobs can be rewarding or it can be perilous. The following checklist can take some of the danger out of it:

1. *Be completely honest with yourself.* Why do you want to change? *Bored with your job?* Remember, it could be *you. Is your boss on your back?* If so, what's the reason? *Your firm isn't moving*

fast enough for you? Don't be too quick to judge your company's future. In many industries jobs exist today where there were none ten years ago. Fifteen years ago there were no such things as automated robot-manufacturing techniques in the automobile industry; today, these offer employees a new field of opportunity. Look at the changes in packaging; not too long ago your take-out hamburger came in a paper bag; now it's in a plastic box; what will it come in tomorrow? Everything is advancing. Before you decide your firm is at a dead end with no future, investigate carefully; talk to company executives. You may find you don't have to change companies to get ahead.

Have you been passed over for promotion? Certainly, this bears serious consideration. Is your firm telling you it might be better to move on? Not always. The choice of the other person may have rested on something far different than capability and may be no reflection against you. Give this one time.

A friend who felt passed over was angry, hurt, and ready to re-sign when I advised him to give the situation at least six months. He did; it turned out that the other person did not work out. My friend was offered the position. Later, he discovered that his very act of staying on had impressed several executives, especially the fact that he had put even more effort into his work.

Before changing jobs, be certain you understand why you wish to do so. When you surrender your ego, hurt feelings, and disappointments, and try to look at your situation through other eyes, you may well find that the problem lies within yourself. If so, changing employment might well be the last thing you should do. Changing yourself can be infinitely more beneficial.

2. *Do you really* know *what you are looking for?* Unless you have fully reasoned this out, you may be like too many men and women I have known who have changed jobs to their dismay. Often they are like a divorced person who remarries to discover that his or her new mate is just like the former one. Without careful study and self-examination, changing positions can put you back in the same frustrating caldron.

3. *Have you sought competent counsel?* There is an old proverb: "The way of a fool is right in his own eyes: but he that hearkeneth

unto counsel is wise." [1] In deciding on a job change, sit down with competent, experienced people and ask their opinions. Often an older person who has been through the mill can point out pitfalls and roadblocks you never imagined.

4. *Beware of your emotions.* Too often people rush into a job change in a burst of emotion; they feel they have been treated unfairly, or the new position sounds "too good to pass up"; or they are simply captivated by "something new." When your feelings run high, that's the time to slow yourself down. Don't do anything until you've considered the new job in the cold light of truth and logic.

5. *Don't burn your bridge behind you.* By all means, do not leave your present job until you have a new one in hand—signed, sealed, and delivered. I have seen too many sad situations in which a person resigned on the basis of a verbal promise, only to later discover that the new job wasn't coming through. This can easily happen when the new firm is in a state of management transition or having financial difficulties. Being unemployed while seeking a job can be rough; remember, *having* a job gives you greater credibility with a prospective employer.

Above all, when considering a job change, surrender your ill feelings against your company, surrender your ego in seeking counseling. Here are two examples of men who made mistakes in seeking new employment and how one was able to salvage his error:

Young Sam Jordan was doing well with his company, a large, conservative firm which had earned the respect of its competitors. However, a dream burned in Sam's heart of someday running his own business. In surveying his talents and aptitudes, he felt he had the necessary qualifications. Most important, he surrendered his dream to the Lord, praying, "Father, I'm willing to do what You want me to do. There is only one place I wish to be: in the center of Your purpose for my life. I know there is no peace elsewhere."

While he waited for guidance, Sam continued doing his best for his firm. Because of the firm's conservative nature, however, promotions were slow in coming and this bothered Sam. It bothered him to the point where he became impatient.

He began surveying the job market. When another company offered him a position that would pay considerably more, he took it. Unfortunately, he had not thought it through nor sought counseling regarding it. The new job turned out to be absolutely wrong for him. Sam was miserable and felt no peace. After eighteen months he and the new firm parted company by mutual agreement.

Sam sat back and surveyed the situation. He took some time for deep introspection. He admitted he had made a mistake, yes. But could this now be the time, he wondered, to realize his dream and begin his own company? Moving carefully and seeking counseling, he began taking one step at a time. Each one seemed right as it led to the next one. Ultimately he launched a financial-planning firm.

During the summer of 1983, while attending a convention in California, I noticed Sam's name on the hotel bulletin board. He was leading a financial-planning seminar in one of the meeting rooms. I stepped into the back of the room and watched Sam finish his lecture to the attending lawyers, accountants, and tax experts. A spirit of joy and satisfaction shone from his face and I knew immediately that he had done the right thing. Later, we had a good talk during which he said, "Lee, I hope I can get the one thought across to others that there's a plan for us all in this life, if we can only be patient so that we can discern it."

Gordon Lustig was another story. He was very good at his work and had an excellent future, but his main concern was himself. Gordon was a complainer. He constantly felt he was being treated unfairly. Whenever we talked he would harp on "not being paid what I'm worth." Actually, I doubt if anyone could pay Gordon what he thought he was worth. On top of this, he kept looking at other people instead of himself, concerned that someone else was getting more attention or being compensated more than he was. Eventually, angry because someone else was promoted to a job he felt he should have had, he quit in a fit of temper. He went to an organization which paid him a salary only two thousand dollars more a year than he had been making.

Gordon's problem continued to haunt him and he ended up in a small firm, heading a minor division. He can always change jobs again. But unless he changes himself, he is at the end of the line, with no place to go.

The checklist of reasons one has to change jobs can be as long as this book. I have mentioned only a few of the more prevalent ones. However, I have saved for last probably one of the worst reasons of all. It has ruined more careers and families, and it is usually the most attractive enticement of all. I call it

The Geographical Illusion

Symptoms of this illusion are such reasoning as, "Oh, won't life be more fun in Florida"; "I'm sure job opportunities are better in California"; "We loved Arizona so much on our winter vacation that I know I could work much better out there."

Knowledgeable members of Alcoholics Anonymous call this ploy the "geographical cure." They have seen too many people suffering from alcoholism who think they can lick their problem by moving to another part of the country. It rarely helps. The sufferer brings his own problem with him.

I knew of a certified public accountant in Milwaukee who tried to overcome his drinking problem again and again. He shrank from seeking the help of a support group such as Alcoholics Anonymous; he felt it was for "weaklings." In searching for an escape, he thought of the mountains of North Carolina where he and his family had often vacationed.

"Wouldn't that be a lovely place to start over?" he asked his wife. "I could open an office and there would be no reason for me to drink." Eager to do anything that might help, she agreed. They moved their household to a small city in the Smoky Mountain area, where he opened an office. Six months later he drove alone one night up into the mountains and shot himself in the right temple.

We Bring Our Problems With Us

The geographical illusion can lead anyone astray, even if he is not trying to escape something. It deceived a young family in Massachusetts who were not having any problems. I'll call them Dick and Jane Brown.

Both husband and wife were working outside the home. He was in computers and she was a teacher. They had three children in grammar school. The trouble began after they enjoyed a lovely vacation in Florida. The two weeks were idyllic. The glistening beaches, soft, gentle surf and warm breezes were a welcome change from the bitter New England winters.

Back home in Boston they couldn't forget that lovely climate as the winter winds whipped snow into drifts blocking their driveway. As Dick fought ice-covered streets on his way to work, he began to sense a feeling inside that perhaps he'd do better in Florida. It reached the point where he began finding reasons for his family to move down there.

More and more his desire was camouflaging itself as reasonable options. He began seeing providential "signs" that he was supposed to go south. While turning the idea over in his mind on his way to work, he'd look up to see an airline billboard advertising flights to Florida.

It's interesting how thoughts gravitate to desires. All that remained was for him to find a job in Florida. And so he began exploring the market. Finally, after several months, he was invited down for an interview and offered a job. Dick did not examine the company carefully. His main wish was satisfied; he had a job and this was his final "sign."

Meanwhile, his wife was not so enthusiastic. She hestitated to leave her friends and family. However, she did not question her husband, feeling he knew what he was doing.

So, the Browns sold their home, packed, and moved. For the first three months it was just as they had envisioned. Then Dick's job disappeared—the company went bankrupt. It had been on shaky financial ground all along and Dick had failed to perceive this. Another job in his field was nonexistent. Worse, his wife could not find a teaching position.

For two years the Browns lived on welfare. Finally, when the Florida economy picked up, he began working again. But the family had been hurt deeply. Dick will tell you that he has learned his lesson. He would like to return north but he knows better than to make any forced move without close inspection and the guidance of others.

Distinguishing Between Desire and Opportunity

This is an actual case history of a man I know who finally learned to distinguish between his personal desire and genuine opportunity in making a career change.

As we live through it with him, you'll note the pitfalls and safe paths he encountered. We'll call him Brian.

Brian was a research chemist with a large food-processing firm in Chicago. At thirty-five years of age, he had been with his company for ten years. Advancement had not come as he thought it should, and he became restless. He soothed his frustration by fishing. It was his most enjoyable pastime, even ice fishing in the winter.

When Brian's firm sent him to the state of Washington to oversee the installation of a new food-packaging line in one of its branch plants, he had some free time to see the area. He was enthralled with the forests and the sparkling rivers. *How wonderful it would be,* he thought, *to live in this region.* Then a few days later he came across a small resort on a lake that was for sale. He could see himself running it while enjoying the great outdoors. Soon he was entranced and decided that he would try to buy the resort and move his family to it.

Danger signal: Brian had fantasized himself into a resort operator. He had allowed his personal desire to override a realistic appraisal.

Brian was so enthralled with his dream that he phoned his wife to tell her about it, then called his father and suggested that the two combine their resources to purchase the resort.

Problem: Brian had no experience operating a resort. In fact he had no business experience in any related field. He was living in an illusion of fun to be had.

Prognosis: Brian would have failed with the resort. In time he would have tired of spending much of his time fishing and enjoying the outdoors and within a few years would have had a miserable life.

What did happen? Brian finally discussed the resort opportunity with knowledgeable friends experienced in the field. He also prayed about it, putting the final decision in the hands of a higher power.

In the end, Brian was given a strong feeling to back off. The good he salvaged out of the experience was finding a wonderful vacation spot to which he could bring his family.

Three years later: Brian was still with the large food-processing firm. And though he had had one promotion, he felt his real career lay elsewhere. Thus he kept his communication channels to opportunities in his field open. One day he learned about a small food company in Maine which was looking for a number-two man.

Here was real opportunity: It was in line with his experience, he did like the food-processing business, and it promised a bright future. So Brian contacted the firm. The president invited him to the plant for a visit. The two hit it off and Brian could see where he could put his ideas to work on behalf of the firm. He was offered the job and accepted.

Result: Brian found real fulfillment and a promising future. On top of this was a splendid by-product: the Maine woods, lakes, and streams providing his fisherman's soul a wonderful outlet. His family was happy, too. Brian, indeed, had found the best of both worlds.

It all happened because Brian had learned the principle of hanging in there. The work to which he had been called through his talent and training came first, over and above his emotional desire, no matter how glowing and inviting it seemed.

Changing jobs might be the very best, or very worst, thing for you. You can only know when you take your time in checking facts and seeking guidance before you make such a move.

Summing Up

The Principle of Hanging in There

1. Do you give your present employment a fair shake before giving up on it?

2. Are you completely honest with yourself about why you want to change? Are the reasons valid or do they stem from your own pride and ego?

3. Do you really *know* what kind of job you are seeking?

4. Have you sought competent counsel in your job change?

5. Don't burn your job bridge behind you. Instead, leave respect and good friends in your previous place of employment.

6. Beware of the geographical illusion: changing jobs in order to move to a favorite part of the country.

7. When wisdom and circumstances indicate it's time to *act*, do so at once.

7

The Principle of
Winning by Losing

Losing one's job ranks high on the traumatic "hit list." Psychologists rate the emotional blow near that of losing one's spouse. A counselor who works with alcoholics told me that, as a rule, an alcoholic will continue drinking despite knowing that his illness will cost him his car, home, and family. "But it's usually the prospect of losing his job that spurs him to seek help," he pointed out.

A job is so vital to a person's self-esteem that when he loses it, he suffers a terrible sense of rejection; he feels that his world has come to an end.

Yet, almost everyone at one time or another has lost a job. And it's not the end of the world. In fact, *it can be the best thing that has ever happened to you.*

Many years ago a young man in New York State had a good job with a bank. He loved his work, but evenings and weekends he pursued his hobby of photography. He developed and printed his own photos, using the old glass photographic plates that were standard for the 1870s. The chemicals stained his fingers, and try as he might, he could not scrub away the blemishes.

One day the bank president called him into his office.

"George," he began, "we like you and you're a good worker, but I'm afraid we're going to have to let you go."

In answering the young man's perplexed look, he continued, "It's those stains, George. We can't have our employees serving customers with hands that look like that."

The crestfallen man walked out of the president's office in deep gloom. His career was in pieces. What could he do now? He glared at his discolored fingers.

Back in his darkroom that night, he bitterly mulled over his disgrace. Looking at his equipment he was vexed by one thought: If only wet chemicals weren't required to prepare plates for the camera.

Then the idea struck him. Well, why not? He had a small savings account. And now he had the time. With a goal in mind, he eagerly went to work. Success came in 1880 when the former bank clerk, George Eastman, manufactured the first dry photographic plates. Five years later he invented the first pliable film. George Eastman went on to revolutionize photography, making it easy and simple for anyone to take pictures using his newly developed roll film. "You push the button; we'll do the rest," became the slogan of the Eastman Kodak Company.

Would it have happened if George Eastman hadn't lost his job?

I doubt it. I have seen it happen again and again: People have lost their jobs and gone on to achieve great success.

Following the Plan

I believe there is a plan for each person's life. We need to find out what that plan is and then follow it.

Take the case of a man who began life many years ago under the worst possible circumstances. Born into a minority race, despised by others who were full-fledged citizens of a powerful nation, he could have been killed at birth. For national law decreed that all new infants of his ethnic background be eliminated. The government felt his group was proliferating so fast that it impaired the nation's security.

However, when he was born his mother shrewdly arranged it so that he was "found" by the government ruler's own daughter. Touched, she adopted him and the baby grew to become a man favored by the ruler and given power and prestige in national leadership.

But the day came when he happened on one of the ruling-class citizens beating a member of his own race. He could have kept calm and used his head, ordering the citizen away and smoothing things over. Instead, he lost his temper and in a rage killed the citizen and hid his body. Word got out, probably from someone in the very minority group he was trying to protect, someone who resented his favored status. As a result, he was immediately sentenced to death by his nation's court. Not only had he lost all position and prestige but he was about to lose his life as well.

He fled the country alone, carrying nothing with him. It was the best thing that could have happened to him. For God had a plan for him, and in order for this plan to be effected, he needed time alone. A time of seasoning. The man's name was Moses.[1]

We have no way of knowing what lies ahead. But the power greater than us knows the answers.

Then there was Joe Rolf, a veteran insurance man who had worked his way up from agent to divisional sales manager of a large corporation. His experience, acumen, and skill made him an excellent man in his field. However, Joe's method of hiring employees conflicted with his firm's philosophy.

Joe's idea was to carefully screen applicants and select only those best suited for the job. The firm's policy at that time followed the "mud on the wall" theory. Applicants were hired en masse. Those who were successful or "stuck to the wall," so to speak, were kept on—the rest were let go.

Joe Rolf's hiring approach cost him two strikes in the eyes of the company. And then there was his wife. A lovely woman and homemaker, unfortunately she did not fit the firm's corporate image. She was not slim, svelte, and a genial mixer at company functions. Of course, this was never mentioned by the firm, but it was there. Joe knew this.

Many corporations are known for quirks about how an employee should act and dress. And not all of them are rational. I have actually heard a top executive admit, "I worry about the temper of a guy with red hair." And then there was the reverse of the normal stereotype when a man told me, "I don't trust a man who smokes a pipe." All too often one man well suited for a position is turned down in favor of another who "looks the part."

And so, Joe's third strike was his wife. One afternoon he was called in by his superior and told to submit his resignation.

Joe did not panic. Praying for guidance, he eventually found another job with a similar company. This time, however, the firm's hiring policy matched Joe's ideas. Also, the company did not demand that wives fit a certain mold.

Joe was soon promoted, and promoted again to senior vice-president. He made a much larger salary than he had previously earned. Moreover, his wife was one of the most popular wives in the company.

What would have happened if Joe had not remained true to his principles? Or if he had tried to force his wife to change her image?

Interestingly, Joe's previous firm, as with most companies, has now come around to the selective hiring approach.

So, if you've been fired, phased out, terminated—what happens next?

How to Get Back at the Firm That Fires You

Many companies have an "immediate dismissal" policy which makes some sense. One New York firm, in reorganizing a large department, fired fifteen employees at once. They were given their notice at eleven o'clock Friday morning, along with four weeks' pay, and told to have their desks cleaned out by three o'clock that afternoon.

Cruel and ruthless? Perhaps. But more and more firms are doing this. Why? Because they have learned that an employee who is allowed to work after he has been given notice can very possibly become a detriment. Disgruntled people have been known to hurt morale by spending their final days criticizing management and, in some cases, sabotaging company operations. By doing this, of course, they torpedo their own value on the job market, for news of what they have done usually gets out.

If you are given the unhappy news that your job is ending and you still have a period of work awaiting you before you leave, the best thing you can do, on your own behalf, is overcome any ill will toward your company. Instead, work each day as if you plan to spend the rest of your life there, working as hard as you can.

For example, Al Whittington was told one Monday that due to a departmental rearrangement, his job would be phased out at the end of the month. At age fifty-four, after seventeen years of service, he was hurt and dismayed. He was tempted to slack off and do little. However, he knew that his department still had to function in filling orders. So remembering, "Whatever your hand finds to do, do it with your might," [2] he threw himself into his work. Naturally, in the meantime he followed up job contacts.

A week before his last day, the head of his department called him into his office. "Al," he asked, "would you be interested in working with a company across town, doing much the same work you were doing here?" Al sat straight up in his chair. "Of course," he answered.

It turned out that the other company needed someone with Al's credentials. An executive who was acquainted with Al's boss had called him and asked if he knew someone he could recommend. Al's superior was quick to remember the man who threw all he had into his work instead of slowing down after being told his job would end as of a certain date.

Perhaps you have lost your job through your own fault. In this case, now is the time to be completely honest with yourself. What went wrong? If you have a problem, now is the time to face it. Perhaps you were not fitted for the type of work you were in. Maybe you have a personality problem that needs rectifying.

Now is the time to seek divine guidance and the advice of friends whose judgment you respect. If they are true friends they will be candid with you. You may also need to see a professional counselor.

I know a man who held four jobs in three years. Steve was a

malcontent. After holding a job for a few months he invariably came into conflict with his superior. "Oh, the guy doesn't know what he's doing," Steve would tell me when we met on the train. Because he wasn't given his way, he became abrasive and ultimately would end up being shown the door.

Not until after several counseling sessions with a psychologist did Steve begin to see that he might be the one who was wrong. When he finally accepted the fact that he had some growing up to do, that he wasn't always right and everyone else wrong, he began to find job stability.

So, you have lost your job? As one who has spent some time seeking employment, let me suggest some steps to take:

1. *Seek guidance.* See a counselor. Seek God's guidance in prayer.

2. *Analyze yourself.* What do you do best? What are your talents? Be honest. I know of a man who was with a large stockbrokerage house. For fifteen years he was never quite happy in his job. Finally, when the stock market had its recession in the seventies, he lost his job. Now was the time, he felt, to do something he had always wanted to do. Antiques were his hobby, so he opened a shop. Today he is doing better than he ever did in the brokerage field.

Think about your hobbies, your talents. The things you enjoy doing are obviously what you do best. It is possible that they might point you to a new career direction. By all means, get help in this. Talk to friends, real friends who are concerned for you. If possible, see a competent employment counselor. A word of caution here: There are many so-called counselors who not only charge exorbitant fees but offer little real help. You may wish to get recommendations from others who have had success with counselors, or check with your local Better Business Bureau.

3. *What do you offer?* Put yourself in the place of an employer and look clearly at yourself. What do you need to improve? What positive areas can you build on? What can you offer an employer that will benefit his business? This is not being egocentric. You're a unique human being and, as such, you have something special to offer this world.

4. *Take action.* Nothing happens unless you *do* something. If you sit at home you will become depressed. Write letters; use the telephone to make contacts. Be sure to keep a time schedule as if you are working. Don't stop getting up early or sit around unshaven all day.

5. *Study the job market.* Where are your skills needed? Scour the job market, answer ads, register with employment agencies versed in the field you are seeking. If you have targeted a particular company for which you'd like to work, find out the name of the executive there who has the power to say yes, and call for an appointment. Don't be bashful. People admire someone with initiative.

6. *Enlist the support of others.* Don't be embarrassed to ask for encouragement from members of your social and church groups. Enlisting the help of others and asking for their prayers places a powerful force behind you.

7. *Step out confidently.* The old adage "Pray as if everything depended on God; work as if everything depended on you," makes good sense.

I learned this as a twenty-four-year-old husband and new father while still going to college. I was laboring on my doctoral degree but it became evident that something had to give—my family or the degree. I had no choice, so I set about finding a job.

I had absolutely no contacts in the business world and no job leads. In 1948 the job market wasn't good. What to do? I wondered. Even then, I believed that it was wise to contact the company executive who was the firm's decision maker. Usually, that meant the president. How best to do this? I knew that a letter coming out of the blue from a stranger asking for a job would be quickly filed by his secretary.

One evening as I leafed through a news magazine, I was struck by a particularly attractive advertisement placed by a large corporation. As I admired it an idea came. *What a great entrée to the president,* I thought.

I tore out the ad and sent it to the president, along with a letter complimenting it. In the letter I said I admired his firm for presenting an ad like this and would like to be associated with such a company. I enclosed my resumé.

Then I got an assortment of magazines, searched through them for ads I liked, and wrote similar letters to the respective presidents. It was simple to get their names and addresses. All it took was a phone call to the nearest branch office or representative. I mailed out two hundred such letters. Within three weeks I had received a large stack of replies ranging from "Thank you very much" to "We'd like to talk with you." One of the first answers came from a company that manufactured adding machines. This ultimately developed into an offer of a job at one of their branch offices.

Elated, Audrey and I, with our little girl, went to Detroit for a brief holiday. On the way I stopped to see a friend who worked in a New York Life Insurance Company branch office. It happened that the office had a job opening and I was so taken with the people I met there that I accepted it. I started with the firm at sixty dollars a month plus commissions, less than the amount the other company had offered. But something told me New York Life was my destiny.

Today I know I made the right decision.

Summing Up

The Principle of Winning by Losing

1. Losing your job can be the best thing that could happen to you.

2. There is a plan for your life.

3. Destiny will out, despite the roadblocks.

4. Always leave good relationships behind you, deserved or not.

5. Analyze yourself. Take advantage of the opportunity to improve yourself.

6. What can you offer that your prospective employer needs?

7. Enlist the support of others.

8. Be imaginative and indefatigable in your search.

9. Step out in confidence.

8

The Principle of
Pain as a Blessing

When Rick Coleman, a computer salesman in his late forties, lightheartedly skipped up the stone steps, he had no idea of what awaited him at the top.

Rick and his wife were walking their small dog in the park near their suburban home that summer evening. When he spied the steps leading up the small hill, he impulsively scooped up the little dachshund and climbed briskly to the top. At the summit his whole world suddenly changed. An empty nausea filled his chest, something he had never before experienced. He slumped to the ground. But after a few moments of breathing deeply, his strength returned and he stood up, thoroughly perplexed.

His wife caught up with him. "What's wrong?" she asked.

He could only shake his head. "I don't know. I've never felt that way before."

Rick forgot about the episode until two weeks later when, while he was walking to his commuter train, it happened again. This time he found himself clutching a tree for support until the feeling passed. Four days later, as he was walking the dog, this time alone, he found himself flat on his back. After struggling to his feet he made it home and collapsed in a chair. His wife rushed him to a nearby hospital, where he ended up in the cardiac-care unit.

A number of intensive tests pointed to blocked arteries leading to Rick's heart. All of the cholesterol-loaded cheese dishes Rick loved so well, the nightly bowls of ice cream, and the every-morning eggs and bacon had caught up with him.

Though his doctor did not consider him a candidate for bypass heart surgery at the time, Rick's life was drastically changed. Instead of the rich, fatty foods he enjoyed so much, he had to concentrate on a fat-free diet. Regular exercise instead of strolls through the park was a must, and he had to shed twenty-five of his more than two hundred pounds. In addition to all of that, he had to remind himself to take pills four times a day and wear a patch on his chest that slowly fed nitroglycerin into his bloodstream throughout the day.

Until now, Rick had enjoyed excellent health all of his life. Except for a childhood tonsillectomy, he had never before been a patient in a hospital. His doctor said he should continue his regular work schedule. This was a real blessing since he had bills to pay and a mortgage on his house. And so Rick joined the millions of working Americans with "heart trouble."

Whether it's a heart condition, arthritis, early stages of cancer, emphysema, or another debilitating illness, sooner or later we all fall prey to the fact of being mortal. I know; I suffered two major heart attacks before writing this book, and then had bypass heart surgery on five arteries.

What do we do? Quit work? Take it easy? Usually not unless we are incapacitated or near retirement age. Otherwise, we find ourselves in the same boat as millions of other working people who are suffering from some kind of illness.

The Power in Not Feeling Well

One day, when I was groaning about aches and pains, a friend said, "Did you know that Winston Churchill once said that most of the work in this world is performed by people who don't feel well?"

"That doesn't make me feel any better," I sighed.

"Well," he persisted, "discomfort seems to bring out the best in us."

"What do you mean?"

He went on to tell about the many people who, despite suffering maladies and illness, have been able to make vast contributions to mankind.

Albert Einstein suffered from severe stomach pain intermittently for thirty years. Though it was diagnosed as a gallbladder ailment, it was never relieved. "When I suffer such an attack," he wrote his old friend and physician Rudolph Ehrmann, "I can often work very successfully. It does not seem to be very favorable for the imagination if one feels too well." Then, in wry humor, he added, "At least the gods seem well intentioned toward me when they squeeze the gallbladder."

Sigmund Freud took Einstein's thought one step further. "I have long known that I can't be industrious when I am in good health," he wrote. "On the contrary, I need a degree of discomfort which I want to get rid of."

And whether one agrees with Darwin or not, we must admire his fortitude. From age thirty-three until he died at seventy-three, Darwin was able to work only a few hours a day on his famous theory. Throughout these years he suffered attacks of nausea, shivering, and fainting spells which required constant rest.

Isaac Newton, who discovered the law of gravity, was an insomniac. And most notably, today, famed British physicist Stephen Hawkins continues to contribute to man's knowledge despite his painful crippling illness which confines him to a wheelchair and makes it difficult for him to communicate. He suffers from amyotrophic lateral sclerosis. The forty-three-year-old scientist has been acclaimed as a rare and authentic genius for his mathematical analyses of space and time in the vicinity of black holes in outer space.

Well-known creative artists, too, have been burdened with maladies of one kind or another at the peak of their careers: Dostoevski, Proust, van Gogh, and Berlioz.

"Could it be," my friend ventured, "that pain and discomfort might help us rise above ourselves? If we were always hale and hearty, might we not become complacent, and rest on our laurels?"

Would Franklin Delano Roosevelt have been able to accomplish as much as he did without suffering polio as a young man? He did not think so. Before his illness, he felt he was a callow young man. Not until he accepted his disability was he able to forge ahead and help lead a nation through economic crisis and world war.

A Blessing in Pain

In fact, the very disabilities that plague us seem to carry their own seed of blessing. Doctor John Bonica, of Mercer Island, Washington, age sixty-eight at this writing, suffers from chronic, excruciating pain. Arthritis and twenty-two operations have left his left leg an inch and a half shorter than his right. He walks with an aluminum wrist cane and cannot stand longer than seven minutes without experiencing terrible pain.

Yet, according to *Time* magazine, Doctor Bonica "is a prime mover in establishing the study of pain as a science.

"Those millions of Americans who suffer from chronic pain have cause to be thankful for Bonica's tenacity," reports the news magazine. "He has helped make much of the medical profession aware of both the compassion and the specialized approach needed to deal with the agony of pain. Twenty-three years ago he helped found the University of Washington Medical Center's Clinical Pain Service in Seattle. This center has since become a model for similar clinics across the country. Here, sufferers from chronic pain can be examined by medical specialists in a variety of fields, from orthopedics to psychiatry, in an attempt to isolate the often mysterious causes of a patient's constant agony.

"Bonica never discusses his own pain," reports the magazine. "He's a tough old son of a gun," says Bill Fordyce, a psychologist at the Seattle Clinic.

Semiretired, Bonica continues to write and lecture and, through his personal example, hopes to prove that a normal existence is possible despite constant pain. After eleven operations to correct arthritic deformities in his hips, he scuba dives, both in

Hawaii and off the coast of Filicudi, the small island near Sicily where he was born.

"If I weren't as busy as I am," he says, "I would be a completely disabled guy."[1]

How a Vietnam Veteran Surrendered

To the best of my knowledge, every case of a person's rising above his disability involves tapping a higher source of power. One of the most notable of these is Max Cleland.

As a high school student Max was a gung ho star athlete out to win the world. In 1967, after graduating from college, he volunteered for service in Vietnam, where he became an infantry captain in the First Cavalry Division. On April 8, 1968, after participating in the battle for Khe Sanh, and with only one month left of his overseas duty, he set out to establish a radio relay station. As he jumped to the ground from a helicopter, he saw a hand grenade laying on the ground. *It must be mine,* he thought. Grenades had fallen off his web gear before. He reached down to pick it up.

There was a blinding explosion.

When Max came to, he stared at his right hand. It was gone. Nothing but a splintered white bone protruded from his shredded elbow. Nausea flooded him. When he tried to stand, he couldn't. Both legs were completely gone.

As his mangled body was airlifted to the nearest field hospital, the medics did not see how he could survive. Shrapnel had perforated his windpipe. He was in deep shock and had lost much blood.

For months Max lay in army hospitals slowly recovering, bitterly replaying the explosion over and over again in his mind, trying desperately to change the ending.

Doctors expected him to become a helpless invalid. But no one reckoned with Cleland's indomitable will to survive. Despite the loss of his legs and arm he was determined to walk again, to swim again, to drive a car, to dance; but most of all, to find a fulfilling career.

He accomplished all of his goals, even to running for political office in Georgia and becoming a state senator. He looked forward to a long career in government.

And then, he suffered an excruciating disappointment when he lost his bid for reelection. In a sense, the loss was even more shattering than losing his limbs. That had been an accident, he reasoned. But losing in his chosen field was a personal, humiliating blow to his self-esteem. Now, his "indomitable" self-will had failed him. Though he had grown up in a Christian home and believed in God, he felt that any accomplishment was up to him.

In debt and out of a job, he sank into self-pity, then deep depression. Finally, he was able to find a staff position on the Senate Veterans' Affairs Committee in Washington, D.C., at a modest salary.

Early on a March morning in 1975 he swung himself into his battered Oldsmobile and began driving up U.S. 95 to the nation's capital.

Weary hours ground by as his car wheels slapped the tar strips and a deep sadness filled him. Why was he still so dissatisfied with himself? He wondered. Someone had once urged him to "let go . . . and let God." But how could one do that and still be in control of everything?

As night darkened the highway, he reviewed his life. He had taken pride in his ability to run his affairs. But actually, how well had he done it? The more he thought about it, the more he realized he had never "let go" of anything in his whole life. He had wanted to always be in control. But how could a person let go and still be successful?

Then, slowly it came to him. Maybe this was a different kind of faith—not a clutching kind, but a letting go. An accepting kind of faith: letting go of it himself and allowing a higher power to take over.

There on Highway 95, as Max stared into the rain-swept night, his eyes began to fill and emotion surged through him.

A deep inner cry of his soul burst through the controlling nature of his will. And as he surrendered himself to a higher power, something happened within him. The tension and frustration

— 112 —

began to dissolve and a deep sense of peace spread through him.

Max continued on to Washington that night. He was a new person. He worked hard at his duties there and learned much about veterans' problems and needs. Two years later he was appointed administrator of the Veterans' Administration by the president of the United States. The youngest man ever to hold that position, he battled for government reforms to benefit particularly the Vietnam veteran. He also became a leader in championing the rights of the disabled. In 1982 Max Cleland was elected secretary of state of Georgia.

It had taken seven years for Max Cleland to learn to let go. And I'm sure that Max, as well as most of us, will tell you there is still some letting go he needs to do.[2]

When I Learned to Give Up

I have been learning to grow through letting go much of my life.

It actually started with my father's death when I was three years old. Though I couldn't really remember him as I grew up, there was that undefinable sense of rejection within me, a sense which I understand every child suffers when a parent dies. Difficult to understand, much less try to explain, a child somehow feels abandoned by the mother or father who dies.

Mother loved and cared for me, of course. But without realizing it at the time I know now that I suffered from not having a father's love. Subconsciously, I suppose, I also resented him for leaving us. And, as I grew older, I believe that this resentment was transferred to almost every man with whom I came in contact.

He was an adversary to overcome. He was a competitor in business, a challenger on the tennis courts, and in every instance, someone with whom to match wits. Even in middle age I did not realize I was still crippled in a man-to-man relationship.

In the summer of 1981, after a New York Life sales conference in Arizona, I went out on the hotel's tennis court to relax. As I lobbed a return shot over the net, I felt a sharp pain in my chest.

Believing it was a temporary inconvenience, I continued playing for two more hours and it went away.

The following winter, after splitting wood for our hearth one Saturday, I stumbled into our kitchen and slumped into a chair, bone tired.

"Lee, you are absolutely gray," said Audrey with concern. "Are you feeling all right?"

"Oh, sure," I replied, shrugging away my weariness.

These were signals. But Lee Buck wasn't listening. I was still driving, trying to win.

A year later, while attending an industry meeting in Phoenix, Arizona, sharp pains shot through my chest. Again, I paid no attention and decided to jog them off. Five minutes later I stumbled back into the hotel, doubled over with pain. Our local general manager rushed me to a hospital, where the problem was diagnosed as angina, or heart pain.

Back home I was given an angiogram which showed some clogged coronary arteries, so my doctor put me on medication.

Again, deciding that no one or nothing would slow me down, I continued working and accepted practically every invitation to speak to church groups, too. These filled all my vacation time and almost every weekend.

I received my comeuppance in March 1983 in Rochester, New York. I was there to speak on Friday evening to a church assembly and again on Saturday morning to visiting missionaries, followed by a morning Bible-study group and a noon men's meeting.

That afternoon I lay down for a nap. Within ten minutes a massive heart attack struck with full force. My entire body was racked with pain. Audrey, her face white with fear, was at my side praying. The pain intensified to the point where I knew I could not stand it. And then something wonderful happened. I found myself letting go of the struggle to win over my own pain. From then on, I felt nothing but peace, perfect peace.

As the ambulance attendants lifted me on to a stretcher, one of the men said, "Don't be afraid, sir."

"I'm not afraid," I said.

I was in the Strong Memorial Hospital for ten days. Six months later I underwent open-heart surgery in which five arteries were replaced. Dr. Richard Shore worked on me for eight hours and that night I groggily awakened in the recovery room, unable to move, with drainage tubes and wires bristling from every part of my body.

There in that darkened recovery room, with its pulsing beepers and winking lights, I surrendered myself finally and completely to God.

As I did this, I realized *He* was my real Father, not the earthly being whom I had resented for leaving me. At the age of sixty, for the first time in my life, I knew the love of a Father. And deep within I was able to forgive my own earthly father—and myself.

A male nurse, thinking that my tears were those of pain, gently wiped them away and tried to soothe me. I could not speak, but as I looked up at him I knew that my old competitive spirit toward other men was finally gone. I knew that now I was able to love other men as brothers.

Ill? Handicapped?

Max Cleland will tell you we are all handicapped in one way or another. We might be suffering from fear and depression, or the grief of bereavement. But as Ernest Hemingway once wrote, "Life breaks us all. . . .and afterward many are strong at the broken places."

Here are some steps we can all take in meeting illness and handicaps:

1. *Acknowledge the problem.* It is difficult, but until we stop trying to change the scenario to make it come out the way we want it, we will never find peace. Remember the serenity prayer: "God, grant me the serenity to accept the things I cannot change, the courage to change the things I can, and the wisdom to know the difference."

2. *Look forward to the new opportunity.* I was in the process of retiring from the New York Life Insurance Company when I had my heart attack. Instead of a calamity, it became a blessing. The Bible says, "All things work together for good. . . ." [3] I found a

new outlook on life and learned to live in peace and tranquillity. As Alexander Graham Bell said, "When one door closes, another opens, but we often look so long and so regretfully upon the closed door that we do not see the one that has opened for us."

3. *Be of service to others.* As the famed British physicist Stephen Hawkins has learned, when we commit ourselves to a positive goal, whether it is solving the riddles of the universe or giving ourselves in service to others, we seem to transcend illness and infirmities. And in this full commitment do we find true meaning and joy in life.

Summing Up

The Principle of Pain as a Blessing

I believe that Max Cleland's favorite prayer, attributed to an unknown Confederate soldier, best sums up this principle:

I was given poverty, that I might be wise,
I asked for power, that I might have the praise of men,
I was given weakness, that I might feel the need of God.
I asked for all things, that I might enjoy life,
I was given life, that I might enjoy all things.
I got nothing that I asked for—
but everything I had hoped for.
Almost despite myself,
my unspoken prayers were answered.
I am among all men,
most richly blessed.[4]

9

The Principle of Asking for Help

How and when we call for help can often make us or break us.

Early in my career I sent up an SOS flag which might as well have been the skull-and-crossbone piracy signal, as far as my company was concerned.

As an eager young agent, I had been sent out as a temporary manager to take charge of a district office that was in trouble. "If you can turn it around by the end of the year, Lee," I was promised, "you'll go to the annual managers' meeting in Florida."

I was thrilled. Attending the managers' meeting was a career highlight; it indicated that you had "made it." Combining business and pleasure, men took their wives to it and I had heard glowing stories about the food, entertainment, and the fun to be had outside of meeting times.

But "turning the office around" was a challenge. Only two months were left until fiscal year's end. I threw myself into the task, working late evenings and weekends. By the end of the year we had made it. The office made its quota.

Excited, I phoned Audrey. "Get yourself ready, honey. We're going to Miami!" Then I went out and bought a tuxedo, which would be necessary for the formal occasions.

The next day a call came from my regional vice-president. "Lee, I'm sorry, but you won't be going to the managers' meeting." He pointed out that it was a matter of protocol, that if one who was not a manager went, then there would be others expecting to go, too. "We've got to draw the line somewhere," he said.

I hung up the phone, seething. I felt betrayed, embarrassed, and very angry.

In short, I was a man who desperately needed help. I needed explanations, comfort, and direction.

Instead, I flew off in four different directions.

Rather than swallowing my pride and sitting down and seeking counsel from the proper person in authority, the regional vice-president who had called me, I got on the phone and burned up the lines to the home office. I sounded off to four different company officers, venting my spleen about the company, its top executives, and its "protocol."

Giving these men a piece of my mind accomplished nothing for me. They were in no position to help or even advise. What did happen was that word raced through the company about Lee Buck's "shooting off his mouth" to everybody.

The blow I struck myself with that bit of self-indulgence was almost mortal as far as my future with the company was concerned. It took me a long time to recover from it.

I had needed help, real help, in a sensitive, critical situation. But my pride would not let me admit it.

This, I believe, is the most common problem in seeking help: admitting that we need it in the first place.

Pitfalls of Pride

We drop the ball, muff an assignment. Our job, household, or personal life is headed for trouble. We're in over our head, and what do we do about it? Seek help? Too often we don't. Our pride will not allow us to admit we have failed or blundered along the line. So we push on, desperately trying to correct it, getting deeper and deeper in trouble until it's too late to make amends or rectify the situation.

Dramatic examples of this unhappy syndrome have been recorded in ship fires at sea, fires in which not only the vessels have been lost but passengers have been injured or killed as well. The cases are tragically classic in pattern.

Usually the trouble begins with a small blaze in a passageway, cargo hold, or equipment room. A crewman tries vainly to fight it with an extinguisher; others battle it and fail. By the time the captain hears about it, the fire is almost out of control. But he will not radio for help, hoping against hope that his crew can contain it. Finally, it erupts into a blazing conflagration and then it is too late.

It is so difficult for us to call for help, to admit that we cannot win by ourselves, that we have failed.

As Somerset Maugham said, "It wasn't until quite late in my life that I discovered how easy it is to say, 'I don't know.' Or, 'I can't do it by myself.' "

No matter what we do, how expert we are, how long we have been handling a task, there comes that time when we can't do it alone. And not until we admit that is there hope.

The Victory of Admitting Need

As an alcoholic or drug addict who has been freed from his addiction will testify, only when he reached the end of his rope and called for help did good things begin to happen.

And it is not just an alcohol, drug, or job problem; it can be anything from inability to handle one's personal finances to succumbing to a sexual sin.

Not until we admit our need is there hope. Then we can take these simple steps:

1. *Sit down in communication with God, admit the need or problem, and give it to Him.* Answers and sustenance will come. No matter how one may describe this "divine wisdom," "intuition," or "plain common sense"—from years of experience I know it is valid and it works.

2. *Open your heart, mind, and soul to this inner guidance.* Ideas and thoughts will come to you. They will be logical and sound. Then it is up to you to *act* on them.

The next point is to *act.* Too often after we surrender ourselves and pray, we sit back waiting for something wonderful to happen—an unexpected check in the mailbox, a phone call with a job offer, a departmental reorganization solving all personnel problems. Life does not work this way. *We* have to step out in faith.

A classic example that has always captured my imagination is the famed World War II air battle for Britain in September 1940. At a time when the country was dangerously short of weapons and the Royal Air Force weak from fighting Nazi bombers, one September Sunday Churchill and his advisers anxiously watched the lights on battle charts in the underground-operations room of the Eleventh Group Fighter Command.

Intelligence reported a heavy invasion of aircraft. And, as the men watched, the chart showed four formations of enemy planes, totaling over 220 aircraft, approaching from different directions.

"The odds were great; our margin small; the stakes infinite," wrote Churchill later.

All they could throw up was a handful of outmoded and worn Spitfire and Hurricane fighters. But the few tired RAF pilots, some making their seventh flight that day, took off.

What happened was a miracle. Some 185 Nazi aircraft were downed in flames, and the heavy strike force turned back. Britain was saved.

What particularly impressed me were the questions asked by some of the downed Nazi pilots who were interrogated after the battle. In awe, they asked, "Where did you get all those planes?"

All those planes?

Some say that phantom aircraft flew in formation with the Royal Air Force that day.

Whatever, I believe the result of that battle represents the power of commitment by those few tired pilots who took off one more time, stepping out in faith.

Another band of weary people who stepped out in faith will also be remembered. When the Israelites who had wandered in the wilderness for forty years were about to cross into the land promised to them, they faced the fast-flowing Jordan River.

God told the leader, Joshua, that when the soles of the feet of the first to cross the Jordan touched the water, the river would dry up before them. Note that the people had to take that *first* step, to actually walk *into* the river. Only then would it become dry.

And step they did. You can imagine the wildly beating heart of the person who hesitantly stepped into those rolling waters—and his shock and relief when his foot struck dry river bottom. Thousands of men, women, and children, along with their animals, followed him across the dry river bottom as the waters were supernaturally impounded upstream until all had crossed.[1]

When we step out in faith, *believing* that we will be helped, dynamic spiritual forces come to our aid.

3. *You might well be led to ask a particular person for help.* This could be your minister, priest, or rabbi. But what if it is your boss, a fellow employee, or even a competitor? Would you shy away from asking? It is a common assumption that few people really want to take the time to help.

On the contrary, most people feel complimented, even honored, when asked for advice or assistance. Something in human nature responds to a plea. That's why most volunteer fire departments and first-aid squads have little trouble filling their ranks.

Not far from my home is Long Island Sound, lined with shore communities. Many have Coast Guard auxiliaries staffed by private boat owners who volunteer for rescue duty. I know some of them. They say there is nothing more stimulating than helping in a rescue. Even towing a disabled boat into harbor gives a special sense of fulfillment.

The Borrowed Bolt

A classic example of the satisfaction people get from helping others happened at the 1964 Winter Olympics at Innsbruck, Austria. The Italian two-man bobsledding team was favored to win the gold medal. Their closest competition was the British team.

As the Italian team prepared to make their final run, it was announced over the loudspeaker that the British team had broken a bolt on a sled runner. "Can anyone help?" rang out the plea.

Eugenio Monti, leader of the Italian team, unhesitatingly offered the bolt from his own sled. After making his run, he rushed the bolt to the British team by runner. With it the British team made a flawless run and captured the gold medal. The Italians came in third. Not until four years later did Eugenio Monti win the gold in Grenoble, France. But in the hearts of everyone, he was already a winner long before that.

It is true. Most people want to help others, especially if asked. There is something appealing about the person who makes himself vulnerable by asking.

On top of that, if the need concerns your work, your superior will have more respect for you if you are willing to admit you need help. You may also know people in the same field who are with other firms. Don't be afraid to contact them. And your competitors? You'll usually find them touched by your willingness to expose an inadequacy.

Moreover, you'll discover that you and the person you have sought out for help will be drawn closer together. When one helps another a special kind of bond is formed.

Winning Together

An old story that bears repeating tells of the man who had the opportunity to visit both heaven and hell. In hell, he stepped into a huge dining hall and saw that the people hunched at the bountifully spread table were thin and starving. Each person had a long iron spoon strapped to his arm from wrist to biceps, making it impossible to bend his arm. Thus no one was able to lift the spoon to his mouth, and all were starving in the sight of the food.

Transported to heaven, he walked into a similar dining hall, where each diner was impaired by the same long iron spoon attachment. However, to his surprise, he found them happy and healthy. The difference was that each person dipped his spoon into the food before him and fed the person seated across from him.

I saw the same principle at work in real life at, of all places, a Girl Scout outing, something with which one who has four daughters is very familiar. On their hike through the woods they came across the old unused stretch of railroad track crossing a large clearing. All of them tried playing "tightrope," walking a rail, but each soon lost her balance and toppled off. Then, two girls boasted they could both walk the full length of the track across the clearing without a mishap. Everyone laughed and said they couldn't do it. At that, the two girls stood up on opposite rails, stretched hands across to each other for balance, and easily walked across the clearing.

A young professional man I know, finding himself in a dead-end job, desperately prayed for some kind of lead to a new position. This happened during the recent economic crunch and nothing seemed to be open.

At the same time the young man became quite friendly with the head of a nationally respected publication covering his profession. The two men frequently walked together from their mid-city offices to the railroad station to catch their commuter trains.

My young friend felt led to tell the other man about his job situation in the event he might come across some opening in the field.

At first he resisted the idea, feeling it might be an intrusion on their casual relationship. Some time passed and still the idea persisted. Finally, he gave in and did apprise the other man of his need.

To his surprise, the man was shocked that he hadn't mentioned it before. "Why, of course," he replied. "I'll do everything I can to help you." And he did. Within a few weeks he passed on information about a company's need for someone with my young friend's qualifications. He is now prospering in a new position with an apparently bright future.

People Want to Help

Often it is a matter of providing advice and counsel instead of a job lead. Persons in authority usually consider it part of their job to encourage and advise young people interested in entering their profession. A friend who is a top editor with a national magazine feels that doing this is a privilege and a responsibility. As a result, new journalism graduates and students in related fields often write him for an appointment—he always makes room on his schedule for a visit. "I remember when I was in their shoes," he says quietly. "I was reluctant to ask an editor to give of his time, afraid he would slough me off. But then as I prepared to visit New York, I summoned courage to write to a magazine editor, asking for an appointment."

He laughed. "I did it, I guess, because I had grown up with that magazine and felt 'at home' with it. Well, to my surprise I received a reply from a senior editor, encouraging me to stop by.

"That afternoon when I walked into their headquarters, I thought to myself that heaven couldn't be any better than this.

"The friendly, silver-haired editor gave me a full half hour of his time and, judging by the looks of his desk, he was a busy person." My friend smiled to himself as if again reliving that moment. "I lived on that visit for years; it helped encourage me to stick with this business. That editor died some years ago, but every time a young man or woman steps into my office 'just to talk about their writing,' I remember that other editor and say to myself, 'Thanks, old friend, this one's for you.' "

Bear in mind that this kind of visit must be confined to information gathering. Seeking a job is an entirely different matter and should be handled with the personnel department or whoever has the responsibility of filling positions.

One Hundred Letters

Seeking counsel is a totally different matter.

I know a young man who did this with interesting results. Peter's lifelong ambition had been to work in book publishing. He loved books, read them omnivorously, and collected them until his parents beseeched him to make some room for the furniture and clothes.

After graduating from a liberal arts college, Peter found a job with a small publishing firm in the Midwest. The job was not satisfactory for a number of reasons, so it wasn't long before he began seeking opportunities in New York, the location of many major publishers.

He started out by writing to one hundred publishers, enclosing his resumé and stating that he would be in their city on such-and-such a date. Would they be interested in seeing him for a job interview?

He did not receive one positive answer.

It was clear that Peter had to rethink his strategy. Part of the problem, he knew, was the recession that was on at the time. But he also realized that asking for an employment interview was the same as asking for a job. Obviously, the editors had no encouragement to offer, or were not in a position to offer employment.

Peter figured that the best thing to do would be to hook into the book-publishing network and become more knowledgeable about the field. He sat down and wrote to top editors of twelve major publishers. In his letter he emphasized that he was not asking for an employment interview but was simply seeking information and advice about the publishing field.

He received eight positive replies.

When Peter arrived in New York, he made phone calls and discovered several other editors would see him on short notice. He had ten interviews that week, four of them over lunch. From these editors he gained a wealth of information which served only to whet his ambition even more, so much more, in fact, that he resigned his job, moved to New York, and began seriously seeking work in the publishing world.

It didn't happen in a day, a week, or even a month. But shortly into his second month he was contacted by one of the editors with whom he had spoken on that earlier visit. No, there wasn't an opportunity opening in his company but he did know of an opening with another publishing house—an opening requiring a specific kind of experience Peter had had in the Midwest. Peter called for an appointment, which was set up for the next day. He was hired, and began work before the end of his second month in New York.

Not only was this method of getting the word out regarding his experience and availability the right way to go but the experience he had in the Midwest was more valuable than he had thought.

One of the attributes Peter had going for him was his sincerity and open-mindedness in listening to the editors he visited. (This undoubtedly was the reason the editor thought of him when he heard of an opening.) People sense this and respond to it. However, if the seeker has a closed mind and attempts to impress his adviser with how much *he* knows about the business, the adviser will not remember him with such a positive feeling. In seeking help, it is letting down one's guard, admitting ignorance, and confessing a need that makes the difference.

In my own work I have had people come to me seeking counseling who, for some reason, built a wall before them. Over the past fifteen years my wife, Audrey, and I have made a home for a number of young women who lived with us at various times when they had no other home.

When one young woman came to us, Audrey and I sat down with her beforehand for our usual talk. We explained that in our house all of us lived together as a family.

"We do not take in roomers or boarders," I pointed out, "and we expect anyone who stays with us to be part of the family.

"We'd like you to be a daughter—a real daughter," I continued. We pointed out the various household tasks she would assume, such as cleaning her room and bathroom, but emphasizing that we did want her to be a genuine part of the family.

She said that was fine and our relationship began. However, almost from the beginning it was not a relationship at all. It was as if we lived in different worlds. After dinner, she would slip off to her room and we would not see her for the remainder of the evening. Despite our attempts to gain her friendship, she went her way and left us feeling we should go ours.

If she planned to be late getting home, she did not call to let us know. One day she lost her job, and this time she came to me for advice. I spent quite some time with her, giving her information and help. But she didn't seem to hear one word. She did not express thanks, and never mentioned our talk afterward.

She finally got another job and life went on as before. In the meantime, Audrey and I were praying about the situation. Finally, we felt we could not maintain the relationship any longer. It was like living with a stranger in the house, one who made it clear that she wanted nothing to do with us.

Finally, the time came when we sat down with her and told her she didn't seem to want to become a part of our family. And, though we loved and respected her, we felt it was wrong for us all to continue in such a situation.

She seemed surprised that we felt as we did and left, still cold and aloof. We continued to love her—and suddenly the entire situation became alive to me as an allegory about our relationship with God.

He wants our company and guides us when we come to Him in fellowship. But too often, we are like that young woman—we do not want this fellowship. We prefer to go our own way. And thus, we fall out of contact with divine guidance and wonder why things don't go right.

Hold Out Your Hand

Julie Harris, the well-known and much-loved actress, discovered to whom she could go for help when plagued with self-doubt and self-condemnation. A crippling perfectionism haunted her and even when she was performing in the Broadway smash hit *Member of the Wedding* it plagued her, stealing the edge from her assurance.

One night she considered herself so inept that she even felt guilty taking curtain calls. On her way back to her dressing room she met Ethel Waters, the star of the show.

"Why, Julie," said Ethel, "what's troubling you?"

In false pride, Julie was about to murmur an "Oh, nothing," when suddenly she broke down and told Ethel how she really felt.

Ethel stood back and looked at Julie with warm compassion. "You're trying to do it all alone, honey," she said. "You know the Lord Jesus, don't you? All you have to do is give those troubles and worries to Him. He'll take care of them for you."

Still, Julie couldn't relinquish her self-doubts and fears. Finally, one day near the end of the play's run, she again confessed to Ethel Waters that she hadn't really made it.

"It's so hard," said Julie, "so terribly difficult to do."

Ethel Waters, her eyes full of love, reached out and took Julie's hand.

"No, it isn't, honey," she said. "Jesus is right with you. If you want the strength and confidence you need, all you have to do is hold out your hand—and ask."

Julie Harris never forgot those words. And every time she felt her old fears slinking wolflike at the edge of her confidence, she would see herself holding out her hand to Jesus for help. "All I had to do was turn to the Lord," she says, "hold out my hand, and receive a quiet confidence and strong assurance that has stayed with me to this day."

Turn to the Lord, our ultimate Source for help.

More than one top executive I know turns to Him, often many times each day. One individual, the assistant treasurer of a large corporation, isn't bashful about relating this.

When someone on his staff comes in with a tough problem, he will sit back and say, "Well, let's get some help on this." Quietly, without fanfare, he will ask God to enlighten them in handling the problem.

Sometimes the employee will join him in prayer. "Other times he or she will be reluctant to admit that one can call upon an invisible Being about whom he has doubts," he smiles. "But more often than not, after a solution has come about, at times in a startling way, they will come back wanting to learn more.

"Usually the answers we get are not miracles," he continued, "but somehow prayer opens our minds to seeing the obvious, to sorting out the essential from the nonessential, to seeing deep into a problem. And somehow, in some way, the answers do come.

"But it must be done in faith. I point out to those who pray with me that we can't be impatient or unreasonable."

He laughs. "I like to think about the man who was given the marvelous opportunity to talk with God. The first thing he asked was, 'God, is it true that to You a hundred million years is just a minute?'

"*Yes,* answered the Lord.

" 'Is it true, God, that with You a hundred million dollars is just a penny?'

"*Yes,* was the reply.

"The man, excitedly rubbing his hands, said, 'Give me a penny!'

"*In a minute,* was the gentle reply."

Summing Up

The Principle of Asking for Help

1. Don't let wounded pride or ego get in your way when seeking help.

2. Call for help before it's too late.

3. Remember that there is always the time when you can't do it alone.

4. When given help, step out in faith.

5. Remember that almost everyone enjoys being helpful.

6. Asking someone for help draws you closer together.

7. Admitting to your superior that you need help usually raises his or her estimation of you.

8. Two people can do the work of many when helping each other.

9. When seeking help from someone, consider his needs and time. Be thoughtful.

10. Communicate with your power source.

—10—
The Principle of Friendship

I'll never forget the dark-haired young fellow I met ten years ago at Chicago's O'Hare Airport. A midwestern blizzard had temporarily shut down the field and we happened to be sitting next to each other in the terminal. We struck up a conversation and I learned he was a middle-level executive with a large mail-order firm.

Our small talk turned into a discussion of the opportunities for young people in the corporate world today. Then he made a comment that gave me a clue to his future. "You know," he said, staring out of the plate-glass wall at the swirling snowstorm, "my dad always said, 'Make as many friends as you can along the way, Joel. They're great security.' "

I knew exactly what his wise father meant, and it was obvious that his son followed his advice. A few years later I saw Joel's picture in the *Wall Street Journal* with the news of his promotion.

Make friends along the way is an axiom anyone wishing success in his work should follow. This means being a friend to *everyone,* all fellow employees above *and* below you, even to those who you feel can do you absolutely no favors.

How one treats others in his or her climb up the ladder is vital. For each friend made along the way is a building block in your foundation of success.

Here are case histories of two men I know. Greg and Dan both began corporate life in their early twenties. Both possessed basically the same education and talent fitting them for their work.

Dan was outgoing and friendly with everyone from the janitor on up. If someone asked him for a favor he was quick to please, and this included helping acquaintances from other firms. The one thing that particularly impressed me was the fact that as he advanced up the ladder he remembered those he left behind.

Greg was a striver. He had little time for making warm, personal relationships unless they were with those who could benefit him in his career. Genial and outgoing with his supervisors, he had no regard for those whom he felt could be of no help to him.

As years passed, Dan had built an extensive network of friends, not only in his own company but in related industries as well. If someone needed a favor, he knew he could call on Dan. Likewise, Dan felt free to call on others. By this time he had advanced to an upper-echelon capacity.

On the other hand, Greg had remained down the ladder in middle management. His supervisors extolled his ability but he was little known throughout the company and hardly recognized at all in his field.

This friendship principle applies to any activity in which you may be involved, from family relations to community and civic work.

Its basic precept, of course, is following the age-old directive "Love one another."[1] It means going out of your way to be nice to or help others, no matter what their station in life. As an old saying goes, "A gentleman is a person who is kind to someone who is of absolutely no use to him."

Look Down and You Must Look Up

It works both ways. For the converse of the above principle is that if you look down on someone who you feel is lesser than you,

you will unquestioningly have to look up to someone who you feel is in higher authority. Thus you become a slave to men.

I saw this principle at work in the life of an advertising executive in a large midwestern firm. He was a despot to his employees and seemed to take pleasure in denigrating them. But by the same token he trembled in the presence of the top executives of his firm, almost bowing and scraping. In total, he was a very unhappy man and not well liked by anyone.

How one treats others on the way up is vital to his future. I was told of an incident which involved a national trade convention being held in San Francisco. One firm was inviting representatives from other companies to a dinner during the convention. A new employee with one of the invited firms had not received an invitation since he had just come on board. His manager suggested he phone the host firm's executive in charge of the dinner. He did, only to be haughtily dismissed with a curt no.

Five years later, the spurned person had advanced to a top management capacity in which he could be of real help to the haughty executive. Do you think he would be willing to help if the need arose? Why should he? He was spurned before and, in his situation, almost anyone else would turn his back. However, knowing the person as I do, he would probably be willing to help the haughty person if asked. That's the kind of individual he is and that is why he will continue to rise to the top.

One doesn't have to become bosom buddies in every encounter. But there are many simple ways friendships can be sparked.

We Can Live on Compliments for Years

There is the spontaneous compliment. One day while walking to my commuter train, I noticed a house owner tending a garden of beautiful roses.

"They're beautiful!" I called out, and he looked up from his work with a grateful smile.

I had forgotten the incident until a few days later when the man and his wife came out of their house expressly to tell me how much my comment meant to them.

"I've been growing these roses for three years," he said, "and you're the first person who has seemed to notice them."

As I walked on I remembered little incidents that have warmed me through the years: a teacher complimenting my crayon drawing to the class, a policyholder telling me how much my explanation of insurance mysteries meant to her.

As someone said, we need food every day to exist, but we can live on a compliment for years.

And then there's empathy, a word of concern to someone who has been ill, a few minutes of sympathetic understanding for one who has suffered a misfortune.

The philosopher Nietzsche said, "When we begin to understand, we grow polite, happy, ingenuous."

Unlocking Reggie Jackson

A journalist friend who interviews celebrities for magazine articles told me how an understanding word helped him in a meeting with Reggie Jackson, the famous home run hitter. My friend had difficulty catching up with Reggie and finally met him at a California hotel where his team was staying for the night. Jackson was under heavy time pressure but agreed to meet the journalist in the hotel coffee shop.

But when the two sat down together, Jackson slumped wearily back in his chair. His face nearly hidden behind big sunglasses, he answered my friend's questions in curt monosyllables. It was obvious the interview was going nowhere.

Adding to the problem were incessant telephone calls for Jackson.

After returning from the fifth phone call, Reggie Jackson slid back into his chair with a grunt. My perceptive friend put down his pen and said sympathetically, "They never let you alone, do they?"

That comment was the key to unlocking the man across the table. Jackson relaxed and sighed, "They sure don't." He removed his sunglasses, looked at the journalist with new interest, and from then on the interview went well.

Jackson responded to the sympathetic comment. Most of us would have done the same.

A Lost Dog

A historical incident involving someone's sympathetically going out of his way for another person took place in 1778 and might possibly have affected the outcome of the American Revolution. During the terrible winter at Valley Forge when American morale was at its lowest, George Washington and Lafayette were conferring in the cold, bare house which served as headquarters for the Continental Army.

In Philadelphia, some twenty-seven miles distant, Lord William Howe, the famed British general and leader of the British forces in America, had returned from hunting in the nearby woods.

As Washington and Lafayette talked, the French general said, "Le General Howe will certainly regret to see spring come since it will mean fighting instead of hunting."

At that, they heard a whine at the door. Opening it, they found a hunting dog, weary and famished. Washington leaned down and stroked the dog's head while asking an aide to get food. Then he noted the dog's collar which was inscribed "Lord Howe."

As Lafayette prepared to leave Valley Forge the next morning, the American general asked his friend to return the dog to Howe. Thus trotting alongside a soldier carrying a white flag, the stray reached British headquarters.

Two days later General Washington read a letter of heartfelt thanks from his British adversary.

Not long after that, Howe resigned his command in America and returned to England, charging that he was not properly supported by his home government. He was replaced by Sir Henry Clinton, who placed his second in command, General Cornwallis, in the Carolinas, and returned to New York. In 1781, Clinton, expecting Washington to attack New York, remained there too long and thus failed to aid Cornwallis in the Yorktown campaign in which the American Revolution was won.

Would the war have ended differently if the famed Howe had remained in charge? And what effect did the return of a loved pet have in General Howe's decision to give up the conflict and return home? We'll never know, but it is interesting to wonder about.

Small acts of thoughtfulness *can* turn the tide in the affairs of men.

Paul French and the Toledo Blade

Perhaps the most important act of thoughtfulness in my life happened when I was just starting out in the insurance business in Flint, Michigan.

Audrey and I wanted desperately to buy a house and finally, after much seeking, found one. The price was ten thousand dollars and we were going to buy it on a GI loan. But we did not have the three hundred dollars for a down payment.

We were sick about missing the opportunity. When I went into the office one morning my face reflected my blue mood. Paul French, manager of the office, was rough around the edges and occasionally used strong language, but he was a compassionate, caring man.

When Paul noticed my mournful attitude he could have passed it off as my having had a fight with my wife, or just having had burned toast for breakfast. Instead, busy as he was, he took the time to ask me into his office.

"Lee, what in the world is the matter with you?" he asked.

"Well," I shifted uncomfortably in the chair, not wanting to admit I couldn't buy a house for the lack of three hundred dollars.

"Come on," he pressed, "out with it."

I told him, admitting I was defeated.

"Lee," he said, tilting back in his chair, "let me tell you a little story.

"There's a steel they make in Toledo, Spain, that's been famous the world over for a thousand years. A sword made of Toledo steel is so sharp you can use it to slice a silk handkerchief in midair, so resilient that you can bend it in a full circle, and so tough you can strike a steel anvil with it without shattering the blade."

He leaned forward: "You know how it gets that way?"

I shook my head.

"The craftsmen take a raw ingot of pig iron, heat it white hot and hammer it, driving out all the impurities. They do this to it twenty-seven times, heating and hammering it until it is pure carbon steel. Finally, they again heat it red-hot and plunge it into cold water. The shock gives it that tempered, hard edge."

Settling back into his chair again, he continued, "Lee, life is a crucible for us all. And it's the hammering, the hot fire, and the shocks that form our character; it puts steel in our backbone."

Then, pulling open a desk drawer, he drew out his checkbook and wrote out a personal check for three hundred dollars. "Here," he said. "You can pay me back when you can. Now get that house. Then get out there and go to work."

Paul French's caring was like igniting a rocket under me and the next month I earned nine hundred dollars—quite a sum in those days. The first three hundred went right back to Paul. But I could never reimburse him for the tremendous boost he had given me. If he had asked me to try and sell insurance to the executives of our rival company, I'm sure I would have tried.

I have never forgotten Paul French. Of course, I wasn't the only one he inspired; he had built up a huge network of friends in the insurance field.

Let me repeat again, to have friends in this life you must *be one*.

An old song says something to the effect that a bell isn't a bell until you ring it, and a song isn't a song until you sing it. Well, love is not love until you give it away.

It's giving of ourselves to others as Washington did for Howe, as Paul French did for me. In the giving we must be sure to clear our minds of prejudices, one of the insidious elements in blocking friendships. Too often, we impute to others undesirable elements that are not there.

"Oh, he's snobbish," we say, or "She looks like someone I wouldn't want to be associated with."

We should not be so quick to judge one another or to take offense. I did just this on the highway recently. While driving home with Audrey from a conference, we entered heavy traffic. Suddenly, a tan car cut me off. I exploded with anger: "Lousy driver! A stupid guy like that should stay off the road."

We continued on and then red taillights glared ahead. It was a tie-up. Finally, all traffic halted and the line of cars ahead of us extended into infinity. People began climbing out from behind their steering wheels to stretch; soon drivers were chatting with one another. I did the same. One man I met at the guardrail turned out to have come from the same conference we had. We discovered mutual interests and struck up a warm conversation. When traffic began to move, we bid each other good-bye and I felt as if I had made a friend. Then, I saw him getting into his car. It looked familiar. It was the tan car!

Afterward during that trip, I was quiet for a long time. The driver of the tan car obviously had no idea he had cut me off. It was my anger that turned him into a villain. When we stepped out of our cars we became friends. The lesson was obvious: When we step out of ourselves and our egos, we can see the good in practically everyone.

Summing Up

The Principle of Friendship

1. Remember to make friends along the way.

2. Be friendly to *everyone*. If you look down on someone, you will be forced to look up to someone else.

3. A network of friends made through the years can be a vital factor in your success.

4. Be glad others feel free to call on you for help, for this usually means there are others on whom *you* can call.

5. Be liberal in handing out sincere compliments; avoid any kind of obvious flattery.

6. Be compassionate to the needs, worries, and problems of others.

7. Forgive your enemies and love them.

8. Remember what Will Rogers said: "A stranger is a friend I haven't met yet."

11
The Principle of Being Open to New Ideas

It's surprising what one can learn from a walk in the woods. This past fall I took my little grandson, Matthew, into a stand of trees behind our house to gather some firewood. After stacking it, we walked back to the house through the brush, and it was then I lost my temper. Both of us were covered with those pesky brown cockleburs that seem to infest every field and brush area where I have ever walked.

I was in no mood to detach them from our trousers and sweaters. Muttering under my breath, I impatiently plucked them off, one by one, wondering how many millions of them I had pulled from my clothes since I was a boy in Flint. I imagined our early ancestors grumbling as I did as they yanked them out of furry skins and hides.

A week later I had my comeuppance. In a magazine I read about another man who, in 1957, returned from a walk in the fields suffering from the same problem. He was George de Mestral, a Swiss. However, instead of grumbling about the cockleburs, he became curious as he plucked them off, wondering, *What makes them stick so tenaciously?*

On holding one under a high-powered magnifier, he found the answer: slender strands with burred ends that securely hooked into a fabric. Nature had developed the perfect fastener. With a mind open to new ideas, he wondered, *Why not try to duplicate the cocklebur and put it to practical use?*

The rest is fastener history.

Today, Velcro brand fasteners are used in thousands of ways around the world and in outer space to secure everything from sneakers to blood-pressure kits to microphones in space shuttles.

There's the difference between Lee Buck, who lost his temper over cockleburs, and George de Mestral who, encountering them with an open mind, noticed something evidently no one else had seen since the dawn of creation.

George de Mestral's attitude is the key to getting those new ideas.

Instead of looking at what happens to us from a "What's it doing *to me*?" standpoint, if we accept the broad view and *see* the inherent possibilities, the floodgates of creativity are opened.

I believe that new ideas are floating around us all the time, just waiting to be discovered. Sometimes we trip over them like Charles Goodyear, who found the key to vulcanizing rubber through a happy accident in his laboratory. Most of the time ideas come to us when our minds, unhindered of preconceptions, are open and relaxed, free of the prejudice that "it can't be done."

Proof to me that ideas are waiting to be discovered in the mysterious universe surrounding us is that sometimes two people, completely unrelated, will come up with the same idea at the same time. Elisha Gray and Alexander Graham Bell, for example, both filed patents for the telephone within a few hours of each other.

Look for the Possibilities

A mind open to our world's unlimited possibilities is free to see comparisons in everyday things that can lead to revolutionary advancements. Sir Isaac Newton's first hint that led to his important optical discoveries came when, in watching a child's soap bubble, he noted the changes of the image that appeared on its rounded surface.

Printing, the invention that changed history, was suggested when someone noticed initials cut into the bark of a tree.

These happy correlations could have not occurred to someone with a closed mind. Again, we must open our minds and give up our ego-centered concept of "having all the answers."

It's so easy for us to take the easy way, to say, "It can't be done." In the nineteenth century the famed physicist Lord Kelvin made these predictions:

"X rays will prove to be a hoax."

"Aircraft flight is impossible."

"Radio has no future."

"Well," you might argue, "who knew anything in the nineteenth century?" All right, let's look at more recent predictions:

"Democracy will be dead by 1950."

John Langon-Davies in
"A Short History to the Future" (1938)

"Television won't last; it's a flash in the pan."

Mary Somerville, radio pioneer (1948)

"Iran will be an island of stability in the Third World sea of change." Institute for the Future, Think Tank (1973)

I believe we are afflicted with a mind-set which can be traced back to too much dependence on what we can see and touch.

The Impossible Bee

We see this in our laws of aerodynamics, which can be used to prove that a bumblebee cannot fly because its wings are too small for its body. Thank goodness the bumblebee doesn't know that.

Some years ago, engineers in the General Electric Company's lamp division used to play a standard joke on young men entering the department. It was like sending a plumber's new apprentice out to search for a "left-handed monkey wrench."

They would order the newcomer to find a way of frosting light bulbs on the inside. They knew this was an impossible job, but it provided the old-timers some amusement until the striver finally caught on to the joke.

But one young engineer never did catch on. His name was Marvin Pipkin, and not only did he find a way to frost bulbs on the inside but he also came up with a special etching acid which, in developing tiny rounded pits in the glass instead of the usual sharp crevices, actually strengthened the bulb.

He had not been told it was impossible, so he went ahead and did it.

Often, it takes strength and determination to see the idea through.

The Crazy Skier

In the years following World War II, a young Colorado skier had a dream of developing a new ski resort in a spot he had found in the mountains. But when he approached bankers and other prospective funders, he was laughed at. "Why, the location you've chosen is right on the road to Aspen, already the most popular ski resort!"

But young Peter Seibert had an inner toughness that stemmed from a previous battle. During his army service, mortar blasts nearly tore off one of his knees. "You'll never ski again," said his doctors. This could have been a death knell to Peter, who had skied all of his life and had earned many championships. But something deep within him kept whispering, *You* will *ski again*. After a long recuperation, he tried his skis and fell flat on his face. It was agony, but he kept at it. A few years later he won the famed Roche Cup race. And so Peter would not let others tell him his dream was impossible. For he had already decided that no tough problem could defeat him. And so he persisted and went ahead to build the famous resort called Vail.

"Sure," you may reply, "Peter Seibert had an idea to follow; all those other successful people had ideas. But what about me? I never seem to come up with anything good."

Well, we can't be like the person who wrote the U. S. Patent

Office asking, "I want to invent something. Please send me a list of things that need to be invented."

That person would have been better advised to send his query to Norman Vincent Peale. For this famed minister and author offers a six-word formula for success: *Find a need and fill it.*

The needs in our world today are staggering. And though innumerable scientists, industrialists, and common, ordinary people are working hard on filling them, they are coming up with only a fraction of the answers.

There are billions of needs out there. And many of them may be as simple to fill as coming up with something like, well, the Velcro fastener.

There are all sorts of ways to find ideas as recommended by psychologists and experts. One is applying an old principle in a new way (de Mestral and his cockleburs). Another is correlating two dissimilar items such as the ball bearing and writing pen into the ball-point pen, or finding a new use for an existing article.

A fascinating example of the latter is one of today's most widely used consumer products. In 1924, the Kimberly-Clark paper company introduced a cleansing tissue for removing cold cream as a disposable substitute for facial towels. Magazine and newspaper advertising showed Hollywood makeup studios in the background calling attention to the new "scientific way to remove cold cream" with endorsements by Ronald Colman, Helen Hayes, Gertrude Lawrence, and others.

In 1929, the firm changed the name to Kleenex cleansing tissue. Then a year later, a company executive discovered that most customers were using the tissue as a disposable handkerchief.

Taking advantage of the obvious, the executive shrewdly switched the firm's advertising emphasis to "Don't put a cold in your pocket," and sales skyrocketed.

The Kimberly-Clark executives did not let their thinking remain in a rut. One of the problems with American railroads was that for too long they kept thinking of themselves as being in the train business. Not until they realized they were actually in the transportation business did their methods improve.

And not until the life insurance companies began to think of themselves as being in the income-replacement business did their real expansion begin. Then new ideas emerged. When life insurance firms saw that policyholders, stricken by illness and unable to work, let their insurance lapse, they offered a new product called "waiver of premium." A kind of insurance on insurance, it kept the policies in effect with cash values increasing during those down times.

It's all a matter of "mind-set," I believe. It's like a person sailing a boat: He can sit back and let his sail luff loose in the wind and go nowhere. Or he can set his sail so that the wind flows across it and gain the power to travel.

The right mind-set comes, I believe, when we tap our source of power and ask for inner strength and peace. Then ideas will come to us.

I feel that ideas come best when we focus on a specific problem. Open your eyes, your mind, your thoughts to a specific need and, sooner or later, you'll discover creative ideas are coming to you.

I know many men who say that some of their best ideas have come to them while shaving. Strange? Not at all, for it is at this time that one's mind, free to roam unfettered, has an uncanny facility for zeroing in on the elusive target.

"But I am not an idea person," one may argue. "I'm not creative." How foolish to settle for such a view of oneself. The Bible tells us that we are created ". . . a little lower than the angels," which implies the tremendous gift we all have been given. Scientists back this up in telling us that we utilize only a tiny percentage of our mental facilities. No limit has yet been found to what we can accomplish.

The Remarkable Rockne

For example, who was Knute Rockne—just a famous football coach? Few know that this gentle, unassuming man who believed in utilizing every resource God had given him was much more than that. Besides coaching five undefeated Notre Dame teams and stimulating national interest in football, he designed modern-day football uniforms and equipment and invented such innovations as the backfield shift.

During this time he worked without assistants, serving as his school's athletic director, trainer, doctor, equipment manager, track coach, intramural sports director, business manager, ticket director, and chemistry instructor. More? He wrote three successful books, including a children's novel, and

- wrote a newspaper column three times a week
- raised in his garden much of the food for his wife and four children, with whom he was very close
- served as a public speaker for Studebaker Corporation
- operated a stockbrokerage firm
- designed the nearly perfect Notre Dame stadium

As I think about his accomplishments, so many of them done quietly and with no fanfare, I wonder if God doesn't send us men like him from time to time to show us that there are no limits to what we can achieve.

How Do I Personally Find Ideas?

1. When I need help, I first pray, believing that I will be given discernment, knowledge, and wisdom.
2. I study the need or problem from all angles, compare it with other situations which might offer insight, and delve into my experience concerning similar needs.
3. Then I make a decision and step out in faith, taking action in the belief that I am following the right direction.

Sure, there are times when I start off on the wrong foot. But if I keep my mind open to the guidance I have sought, I usually am nudged to the right path.

Beware of Overanalysis

One of the problems I find in corporate activities, whether they are in industry, community, or church, is overanalysis of ideas. Too often a large group of people will be involved in formulating a program or coming up with an idea. And what results, more times than not, is overanalysis, which can paralyze thinking and decision making.

Too often in the insurance industry I have seen a good product suggested, only to have it go into committee, where it is analyzed, dissected, and argued to the point where, when it is finally introduced to the public, the market for it has long passed.

Two or three people can usually get together on a project and come up with a viable plan in a relatively short time compared to the painfully slow deliberation of a large committee.

Drawing Ideas From Other People

The corporate executives I have known who have followed the principle of servanthood and care for their employees as brothers, usually find a steady flow of good ideas coming from them.

Japanese firms long ago learned this vital principle of productivity through people by instilling in every employee the knowledge that his best work and ideas are vital to the success of the company.

Who Gets the Credit?

Concern about who gets the credit for ideas can be a pitfall in any organization.

Some years ago at New York Life I was placed in charge of planning the annual top sales awards convention, one of the major meetings of the year. At the time I was a vice-president working for the senior vice-president of marketing. To begin, I gathered a group of agents from the field and home office for a discussion in which we came up with some novel ideas. One of them was to set up a colorful row of state flags behind the block-long speakers' table. Each agent who had earned an award would be represented by his own state flag which, along with the others, would have its own special spotlight.

It turned out to be an excellent meeting with a lot of pizzazz and showmanship. At the final meeting, the agent who was master of ceremonies that day stood up to praise what he called "the most outstanding meeting New York Life has ever held."

As I sat there fully expecting to hear myself praised, the agent went on to give full tribute to the senior vice-president, who really had nothing to do with planning the meeting.

I sat at the table, stunned. Sick with disappointment, I fell into a blue funk. I was so angry and upset I wanted to go home. However, the senior vice-president had a reception in his hotel suite that evening and I had to make an appearance. But I stood sulking in a corner, not saying a word.

Of course, this was before I learned how to tap my power source. Otherwise I could easily have passed it all off with a quick thought such as, *Okay, the work was a success, it pleased a lot of people, and that is what is important, not who gets the credit.*

Today, I realize that the reward one really gets for coming up with a good idea is not accolades from his peers or superiors. It is, instead, the warm, inner joy one feels when he knows he has done his best, and when he has done it to serve others.

I know that in life we *are* rewarded for our efforts in ways we cannot imagine at the time. The reward may come later, but it will come in a most beautiful way.

When your priorities are right, you work for others, doing your job with all your might. And the joy you'll reap in return cannot be gained in any other way.

In closing this chapter, I would like to point out that one does not have to travel far afield to get those great ideas. Too often we feel that another company, another part of the country, will lift that magic curtain to success.

Many years ago a midwestern farm boy felt this way. Like many aspiring artists he yearned to be in Paris. In time he got there. He lived on the Left Bank, attended art classes, haunted museums, even grew a beard and wore a beret. But nothing much happened with his painting.

After returning home to the Midwest, his career took a turn. He began to paint people and scenes familiar to him: his mother, farm landscapes, and plowing views.

One day he used an old farmhouse as a background for a couple representing a father and his spinster daughter. As a model for the father he used his dentist, and to represent the daughter he asked his sister to pose.

Today, as with most of that artist's midwestern paintings, this piece of art is world famous: *American Gothic* by Grant Wood.

Summing Up

The Principle of Being Open to New Ideas

1. Look at happenings from the broad view instead of just "What's in it for me?"

2. Free your mind of the prejudice that "it can't be done."

3. Look for comparisons—outlandish as they may seem—in everyday things. Remember the cocklebur and the Velcro fastener.

4. Attain that childlike vision to see the inherent possibilities in everything that affects you.

5. Look for possibilities in applying an old principle in a new way.

6. Be alert to combining dissimilar objects or thoughts in creating a new and beneficial result.

7. Recognize the great source of creativity in yourself.

8. Avoid overanalysis and undue emphasis on committees.

9. Recognize that ideas are often close at hand.

10. Remember the winning formula: *Find a need and fill it.*

—12—
The Principle of Communicating Your Ideas

How often have you seen it happen?

Someone is trying to get an idea across to another person, perhaps suggesting an improvement in his work or personal life. As well meaning as the adviser may be, the scenario usually follows this unfortunate line:

"Let me tell you the right way to do it."

The listener struggles to indicate interest.

"You see, you've been doing it all wrong."

The "student" slumps in his chair and stifles a yawn.

"I've had quite a bit of success with this method and if you listen closely, I'll explain it."

The subject's eyes glaze over.

The problem? Most people resist new ideas. It's human nature to *not* want change. And even if one is open to suggestions, teaching him through the "lecture method" usually doesn't work.

One reason for this is that most people who are listening to a person tell them something usually do not really hear them. They are thinking about what *they* are going to say in return—their ideas, their questions, their objections to what the other person is trying to tell them.

How can you get their full attention?

Participation.

People learn best when participating on a one-to-one basis with the teacher. And the best way to bring a person into participation is by asking him questions. We discovered this in the life insurance business. For years managers used to train agents by *telling* them what to do. This never worked out well because:

1. The manager *telling* the agent what he thought the agent should know was a one-sided communication, with no give-and-take.
2. Though the agent may have had problems the manager didn't know about, he wasn't encouraged to reveal them in a one-sided relationship.
3. In his focusing on *telling* the agent what to do, the manager might well have missed discovering information about the agent pertinent to the problem.

To remedy the situation, an older manager and a young vice-president spent two years developing a new system of field-management training techniques.

Basically, they came up with a question-and-answer technique. Instead of telling the agent what to do, the manager asked questions that prompted the agent to think, analyze, and come up with the right answers himself.

For example, let's take the case of a new agent who has been out in the field all week and hasn't sold a policy. Naturally, he has kept records of his calls and activities. The manager and agent sit down together in a quiet restaurant or a pleasant office and begin talking.

The manager starts by asking caring questions about the agent's family or other aspects of his personal life. These preliminaries are to encourage a friendly relationship in which the agent senses that the manager has his best interests at heart.

Then they get down to business (naturally, the following conversation has been substantially condensed).

MANAGER:	Jack, tell me what you did on Monday, your first day.
JACK, THE AGENT:	Well, I spent two hours phoning people and didn't get a single appointment.
MANAGER:	Hmmm, that's too bad, Jack. Tell me, what did you say on these calls?
AGENT:	I told the prospects that I had some interesting proposals to tell them about life insurance.
MANAGER:	Why did you say that?
AGENT:	(*scratches his head*) Well, I wanted to get them interested in what we had to offer.
MANAGER:	(*kindly*) Do you think it was effective?
AGENT:	(*laughs*) No. If it was, I would have gotten some action.
MANAGER:	Well, what do you think you should have said instead?
AGENT:	(*ponders a bit*) You know, I should have been more specific. I should have come up with something to excite the prospects' interest. (*Agent thinks some more.*) What with all the consumer interest in investments these days, I should have told them about our Single Payment Premium plan which would not only earn them excellent interest but benefit them through life insurance coverage at the same time. (*Agent slaps his knee and moans.*) *Now* I think of it.
MANAGER:	Congratulations, Jack! You've come up with a fine telephone idea; do you think you'll try it in the future?
AGENT:	(*excited*) Today, in fact.
MANAGER:	Are you willing to write this idea out for us? I'd like to pass it on to the other agents.
AGENT:	(*glowing*) Sure, I'll have it ready for you this afternoon.

The conversation continues.

MANAGER: Now, did you have any personal interviews with prospects that Monday?

AGENT: Yes, two.

MANAGER: Tell me what happened in the first interview.

The manager follows this up with a number of questions, such as:

Who was the man you called on first? How did you get his name?

What did you know about him beforehand?

How old is he? What kind of work does he do?

What made you think he was a prospect?

What did you say about our various insurance programs?

When the manager perceives that the agent has used the wrong approach, he asks:

Did you think that was the right thing to say?

Did you notice the man's reactions?

As the agent considers these questions, he is forced to think and to come up with new ideas and improved techniques. The vital difference is that the agent himself generates the new thoughts and there is no more powerful motivator than a self-inspired idea.

Questions That Care

To best help people in this manner, the manager must give up his natural belief that he "knows it all," that he is the boss. Even though he's quite sure that he's a most capable manager, he must admit that he can still learn a great deal by asking questions. We have found that people love to be asked questions when they think they might be able to be of some help. This guiding-thought-question technique can be helpful in any relationship—parent-child, teacher-student, foreman-apprentice—yes, even spouse to spouse. But it will always take cooperation on the "teacher's" part. We must suppress our natural desire to *tell* the other person what to do, even when we're convinced we know best.

The truth is that the individual probably already well knows what is right in the situation and realizes what he should do about it. In answering caring questions, he is stimulated into discernment, understanding, and action. By the same token, the questioner learns something also, for this seeking process opens up his own mind and helps him sense his own true motives.

In pondering and evaluating the agent's answers, his own creative processes are stimulated. This same technique can be employed when addressing an audience. When you want to spark attention, ask a rhetorical question such as, "Now, what do *you* think of *that?*"

Questions That Inspire

A friend told me how the question method inspired him to accomplish a significant coup when he headed the public-relations department for a national chain of stores. The firm planned to install a large new store in an important location, representing a heavy investment. It was vital that the store begin operations in the best possible manner.

The firm's vice-president in charge of real estate took my friend into his office and explained the need for the best store-opening send-off. Then, instead of demanding, "You get out there and get loads of publicity," the vice-president asked, "What do you think you can come up with for us?"

My friend says that the question was a tremendous stimulant. Instead of laboring under a whip, he felt as if he had been entrusted with a vital responsibility.

He dove into the challenge, and after some weeks of intensive research discovered that the store location was the site of the city's first dwelling. This historical landmark had never been located before and, in itself, made headline news in the community. A bronze marker plaque with significant details was designed by my friend and mounted on the exterior of the store building. It was unveiled at grand-opening time by the firm's president, along with descendants of the first settler, and generated loads of publicity.

It very likely would not have happened if a wise man hadn't known how to place the ball in the publicity man's hands so that he was inspired to run with it.

Proper communication is so important. A survey of some three thousand successful men and women showed that if you can't communicate, you cannot get your ideas across.

The Executive Ear

John T. Molloy, business consultant to scores of large firms, says that "great communicators are all listeners, listening carefully, patiently, even kindly. They encourage people to speak to them. They hardly ever step on a man's ego or a woman's sentence. Even if they don't like a suggestion, they treat it with respect and the people coming to them with respect. The really great communicators are great receivers as well as great senders of messages."[1]

Of course, there's always the time when you'll be on the other end of the line, trying to sell someone your idea.

Whether you're trying to sway a higher-ranking company official on a new operating procedure or motivate a church committee on using a new Sunday-school curriculum, you are facing an age-old problem. For, as stated earlier, people as a rule shrink from new ideas. They don't like change.

So *before* presenting your proposal, find out how it will affect others. Can you come up with something that will make it attractive to them? What might be their objections? If you can find this out beforehand, you might be able to make your idea more palatable before proposing it. Try to discover the needs and thinking process of the other person *before* you try to sell him on something.

Find out who else might be involved in your proposal. If it's for a new office system, check with those involved first for their ideas. Encourage them to point out problems. Then be sure to give them credit for any suggestions they have. When you give everyone concerned an opportunity to become involved in your idea, it already has a powerful head of steam behind it.

When your idea is successful, be sure to share the credit for it. Make sure everyone knows who was involved. There is no better way to keep other people on your side. Who knows when you'll need their help again?

One of the Greatest Salesmen of All

When it comes to getting ideas across to others, I believe we need look no further than a man named Paul who hailed from the city of Tarsus. He probably did more in spreading Christianity throughout his world than anyone else. And, as a marketing man, I have always been impressed by how he sold this new concept of God to some of the most sales resistant people on earth.

The people of Athens, Greece, were not only highly sophisticated and erudite but also felt they knew everything there was to know about the gods who ruled the earth.

When Paul strolled the teeming streets of Athens, he knew what he was up against. He could either be soundly ridiculed or, even worse, ignored. So before addressing his customers he did what every good salesman should do: He carefully researched his clients' needs and their life-styles.

Finally, he was ready to make his presentation. He chose Mars' Hill, a gigantic gray rock mount which still rises adjacent to the great Acropolis and the stately Parthenon. He had little trouble gaining attention. Athenians were always ready to listen to someone's ideas. But if they detected anything phony or inconsequential, you can be sure the speaker would be quickly ignored or hooted out of town.

"Men of Athens," began Paul, "I perceive that in every way you are very religious."

Wonderful. He immediately struck a rapport with his listeners by complimenting them on something close to their hearts.

"For as I passed along, and observed the objects of your worship, I found also an altar with this inscription, 'To an unknown god.'"

It's easy to visualize the Athenians nodding their heads: Since they were not sure they had included all the deities in their divine roll call, this altar was one way of hedging their bets.

"What therefore you worship as unknown," continued Paul, "this I proclaim to you." And so he launched into an erudite and logical witness to the God who created the world, giving him the opening through which he brought Jesus and the Gospel naturally and effectively.

Though a few mocked Paul when he spoke of the resurrection of the dead, others said, "We will hear you again about this," a marvelous compliment to an unknown speaker from out of town. And some of those men joined him and became believers.[2]

Paul's success was based on a method by which he concerned himself with his audience's basic interests and gained their attention so they would listen with open, unfettered ears to the living message of Christ.

How successful was he with those Athenians? We don't really know. But we do know that today in modern Athens at the bustling intersection of "Avenue of Dionysius the Areopagite" and "St. Paul's Street" below Mars' Hill, his sales message for the eternal kingdom stands there on a bronze plaque.

Certainly, Athens was known for its famous philosophers, such as the great Socrates. But I believe more people the world over are familiar with, and live by, the off-the-shoulder remarks made by a traveling tentmaker called Paul.

When asking questions, remember to make others aware that you:

- sincerely want them to speak up
- recognize the importance of their views
- want to hear them out fully
- won't take personal offense when their views differ from yours
- value a person who makes his views known by reflecting this in your attitudes and actions

Stepping into the other person's shoes is the best way to communicate with him. I always remember the old legend about the man sitting in his snug living room one evening as a blizzard raged outside. Suddenly, his windows rattled as a flock of storm-driven sparrows fluttered against them. He stepped out to find them huddled in exhaustion on the sills and porch floor. His heart went out to them and he trudged through the snow to his warm barn, opened its doors, returned, and tried to shoo the sparrows to the barn, where they would find warmth, grain, and rest. Of course, they fluttered away from him in fear.

He thought, if only he could become a sparrow for one minute, how quickly they would listen to him.

Summing Up

The Principle of Communicating Your Ideas

1. Gain your listener's interest by getting him or her to participate in the idea you're offering.

2. Ask questions, encouraging your listener to come up with his own suggestions.

3. Let go of any belief that you know it all.

4. You will be surprised at how much you learn from your listener.

5. Uplift your listener's sense of self-worth. Encourage him to contribute ideas.

6. Be sure *you* are communicating. If your listener does not understand you, how can you help him?

7. Try to discover the needs of the one you're trying to help, or who you want to help you. You'll gain an ally.

8. Share the credit. It's money in the bank for future cooperation.

9. Always, *always* put yourself in your listener's shoes.

—13—
The Principle of Speaking With Authority

Whenever I hear about someone "speaking with authority" I remember the voices I heard almost every evening in my boyhood neighborhood. As the supper hour drew near, a mother living near us would lean out her front door and plaintively call, "Johnneeee. . . .supper time."

Johnny would never answer her. He would usually be involved with the rest of us boys in touch football and his mother might as well have been a whippoorwill calling from an elm tree. Her plea would build in intensity "Johnneeeee. . . .you come here, right this minute!"

As if he had ears of stone, the red-haired boy would concentrate on whoever of us was trying to get past him with the football. Finally, the door would bang shut. Then another voice would sound. This one was deeper, quieter, and sounded one syllable: "John."

The red-haired head would jerk up; tossing the football to one of us, he'd blurt, "Got to go, guys." And off he'd dash.

The same thing happened every evening. And even at our young age we knew the difference between the two voices.

Johnny's father spoke with authority. His mother did not.

Though she cajoled, wheedled, and even threatened, he knew there was little substance behind her entreaties.

But when his father called, he knew he'd better get home, or else.

The difference, I believe, lay in the fact that Johnny's mother had not really committed herself to getting her son home. Her mind was more on the potatoes boiling on the stove and the baby needing changing than on Johnny. Subconsciously she did not *expect* him to obey her.

On the other hand, John's father had one goal in mind. *Get the kid in the house.* He *expected* his son to come home and his voice reflected this.

This is a lesson I have long remembered, and I have watched it at work in many group discussions. There is the timid person who doesn't seem quite sure of his premise. Conversely, there will be the man or woman who talks too much, or too loudly, and who often leaves the same unsure impression. There is the pushy, aggressive person who usually triggers a red flag in the minds of the others.

Then there is the man or woman who quietly makes his or her views known in a low-key manner. This is the one to whom the group usually listens. For this person projects confidence, a sense that he knows what he is talking about.

The Timbre of Authority

The low-toned, serious-sounding voice is the one to which others usually listen. In reflecting on this, John Molloy, a well-known adviser on success in the business world, reports that 95 percent of American males can boost their voice power by lowering their speech tones from a half to a full octave. He says that the same percentage of women can do it, too, by not only lowering their voice tones one full octave but by slowing their speech as well. He claims that too many women tend to speak too quickly, thus losing their effectiveness.[1]

However, I believe anyone can speak with authority, regardless of the quality of his voice. How does this happen? One must speak from a position of credibility on the subject under discussion if he is to be taken seriously. If you hear three women discussing how to raise children and you learn that one is a childless person, another is an older woman who never married, and the third a grandmother, there is no doubt as to whom you would listen.

Being prepared is absolutely essential! One of the greatest speakers of our time, Winston Churchill, whose very rhetoric helped save his nation, recognized this very well. I heard a story from a friend who, while touring the great statesman's office quarters in London, noticed that one part of the carpet in front of a full-length mirror was well worn as if from much pacing back and forth by someone.

"That," pointed out the guide, "is where the prime minister practiced his extemporaneous speeches."

Speaking with authority, however, goes much deeper than voice octaves, points of view, and practice. It stems, I believe, from the speaker's strength of conviction, which gives him that quiet sense of confidence so powerful in moving people.

I am certain that this is the point at which tapping your power source becomes important. If, instead of depending on your own skill and intelligence, you have sought guidance from your power source, you can step forward with the certainty of having a spiritual authority with you. This, I feel, endows one with an air of quiet credibility that others respect.

Sea Drama

As an example, we have only to look at a two-thousand-year-old historical case in which the lowliest person in a large group of travelers, many of them powerful leaders, rose to command the entire expedition within two weeks.

When the Apostle Paul began that dramatic voyage from the port of Caesarea to Italy, he had long since surrendered his life to his Lord. Accused by Palestinian authorities of breaking the law, he adroitly escaped from their clutches by appealing to be judged by Caesar, his right as a Roman citizen.

And thus it was that along with his companions Luke and Aristarchus, the gray-bearded prisoner of a Roman guard commanded by Julius, he boarded a giant Alexandrian grain ship bound for Italy. With its 276 passengers, including crew, centurions, and prisoners, the ship set sail, only to be buffeted by contrary winds. It finally worked its way into the Aegean Sea, where the ship anchored in a bay called Fair Havens, on the south coast of Crete.

It was here that Paul, a veteran marine traveler who was well acquainted with the unpredictable fall weather of the Mediterranean, advised the captain to stay in port through the winter. However, the captain chose to gamble on a forty-mile run west to a larger wintering port. This was a mistake.

A vicious northeaster caught the ship in midsea. For ten days, lashed by a powerful gale, the ship pitched and rolled amid mountainous green waves. Lost, with no bearings in the pitch-dark storm, the terrified crew heaved everything loose overboard. Finally, everyone, including the seasick captain, gave up hope and prepared to die.

It was then that Paul, steadying himself against a mast, calmly urged everyone on board to take heart. As the others lifted their heads in wonderment, he told them that his God had assured him through an angelic visitor that not one aboard would die, though the ship would be lost.

Here was the lowliest man aboard ship, a prisoner, making an unbelievable claim. Yet records show that the others *listened* to him. For it is clear that they responded to the certainty in his heart, a certainty given Paul by his strong belief in what he had been assured. Encouraged, the crew resumed trying to save the ship. And on the fourteenth day of the gale they sensed through soundings that land was near. Heavy anchors were thrown out to steady the ship and keep it from crashing on the shoreline rocks.

Then, either through catching the gleam of white surf or lamplight in the distance, they saw that indeed they were very close to land. At this, all discipline fell apart and the fear-stricken crew endeavored to escape to shore. "We'll lay out bow anchors," they lied, as they lowered the ship's big lifeboat.

Paul, discerning what was really going on, called out to Julius, the centurion who was guarding him. Pointing to the fleeing crewmen, he said, "Unless these men stay in the ship you cannot be saved."

Sensing the authority in Paul's voice, the veteran military leader obeyed immediately and ordered his troops to slash the lifeboat's ropes with their broad swords. It crashed into the sea empty, to be splintered by the waves.

As the fourteenth day dawned, Paul, who had boarded as a despised captive, was now in charge of the ship, giving orders. He urged everyone to take some food for strength, as they had not eaten since the storm broke; ". . . not a hair is to perish from the head of any of you," he reminded them. After watching him take bread, give thanks to God for it, and then eat it, they followed suit.

Soon, feeling able, everyone took practical measures to help save the ship, even throwing the wheat cargo into the sea.

As day brightened, they noticed a beach within a bay ahead, and chopping away the anchor ropes, they let the ship drive toward shore until its bow grounded on a sandbar. It was the island of Malta.

As the pounding surf began breaking up the ship's stern, the Roman guards unsheathed their swords, ready to kill all prisoners to keep them from escaping, normal procedure for that time. However, Julius, their captain, remembering Paul's admonition that everyone would be saved, ordered them to let every person go free. And all 276 people, some swimming, others grasping planks and debris, made it safely to shore.[2]

The Authority of Surrender

None of the passengers would have been saved if Paul had not been there, speaking in quiet tones of authority, an authority stemming from his complete surrender to God.

One of the reasons Paul was able to so effectively reach his listeners was that he was obviously speaking to their common good. When people sense a speaker is for them, they listen. The passengers and crew listened to Paul because he was trustworthy.

"I'll trust you as long as I believe you have my best interests at heart," is the unspoken challenge every person flings at his leader. No person can lead others who do not trust him.

A highly respected businessman made a statement I'll never forget: "People like to work for a leader who is fair and square in every respect. It's a pleasure to work for someone you can trust, always a problem to work for someone you can't.

"Leaders who want to enjoy this kind of reputation have to *earn* it. This first step is to make up your mind to show the same consideration for everyone, regardless of whether they are weak or powerful, loudmouthed or mousy, a personal friend or someone you don't like very well. Run a fair ship without favorites.

"And don't try to kid anyone. Call a spade a spade, say what you mean and mean what you say. People don't like double-talk. They prefer a leader who gives them straight facts—even when they're not very pleasant. It's a lot better than a manager who tries to gloss things over and make black look white.

"Be obvious, simple, straightforward. When people know for sure you're being fair with them, there's a good chance they'll be fair with you."

Another term for this is *servanthood*. A leader must be a servant of those he leads. Paul exemplified this in all of his endeavors. As a servant to the passengers and crew on the ill-fated ship, he became commander of the situation and all lives were saved.

"Whoever Wants to Be Great"

As Jesus said, ". . . whoever wants to be great must be your servant, and whoever wants to be first must be the willing slave of all."[3]

Servanthood is being supportive, encouraging others to do their best. Paul encouraged his fellow passengers by saying they would arrive safely, as they did. He focused on the objective, not the objections.

Too often we focus on the objections instead of the goal. The winner of the hurdle race does not see the hurdles when he begins his run; he has only one thing in mind: the tape at the finish. He knows the hurdles are there, but he focuses on the goal.

On the ship Paul could easily have focused on the hurdles—the drawback that he was a despised prisoner without authority. Instead, he focused on the common good—the saving of all their lives.

Too often we hear the whining complaint "But I don't have the authority." The real problem is that people *do* have the authority if they would only exercise it. They do not because they fear they may make a mistake and be criticized for it.

A Daughter Marooned

Some years ago I had a personal experience with the problem of authority.

My family was living in Atlanta and our daughter, Merrilee, then sixteen, had been visiting a friend in Connecticut during the Christmas holidays. On her way to La Guardia Airport to return home, the airport limousine halted at a way stop. She stepped out to buy some candy. When she arrived at La Guardia she discovered she had left her purse, containing her airline ticket as well as her money, at the way stop.

A blizzard was raging outside the terminal. Frightened and confused, Merrilee telephoned us collect, using a dime she had in her pocket. I told her to go to the airline counter to wait for word from me. Then I phoned that airline in Atlanta, seeking to pay for her ticket so she could get on the plane in New York to return home. "I'm sorry," was the answer, "but I don't have the authority."

In deep concern, I phoned the airline's ticket counter at La Guardia. Wasn't there some way I could expedite funds to them to see that my daughter got home safely? I asked again and again. "I'm sorry, I don't have the authority," was the reply.

Finally, in frantic desperation, I called the president of the airline. "Don't worry," he assured me, "I'll handle it." Within the hour Merrilee was on board a jet, with a loan of twenty-five dollars to see her to Atlanta.

The president of that airline was astounded that someone at his company's ticket counter in both New York and Atlanta had not gone out of his way to find some alternative for remedying what had become a frightening situation for a sixteen-year-old girl.

Shortly after this, the same president sent a memorandum to all employees stating that their airline was in business to serve people and if a passenger had a problem it was their business to help in every way possible.

A Journey of Love

Then we have an employee of another airline who did exercise her authority in another desperate situation. Elisa Vazquez was sitting at her desk in the airline's New York offices well before working hours began, when a phone started ringing. Since the office was still closed, she decided to finish her cup of hot chocolate. However, when the phone kept ringing, she went over and picked it up. It was a grandfather in New York with a heartrending request. He had a three-year-old grandson in Los Angeles whose parents had been judged unfit to raise their child because they were drug addicts. The child would be placed in a foster home unless he could be flown to New York. The problem was that a child this age could not fly unescorted—and the grandparents had been able to borrow only enough money for the child's one-way ticket to New York. The grandfather was sobbing.

It looked hopeless until Elisa exercised her authority.

"Look," she told the weeping man, "tomorrow's my day off and I can fly to Los Angeles and back for next to nothing. I'll pick up your grandson for you."

Early the next morning she met the boy's grandparents at Kennedy Airport before leaving for Los Angeles to get the boy. The grandmother hugged her. "I don't know why you're going to so much trouble for us, Lisa, but God's love is surely working through you."

Yes, His love started working through Elisa Vasquez in a bold way when she took authority in the situation. It would have been easier for her to tell the grandfather that it was out of her jurisdiction, but she stepped out in the true sense of faith.

The Oration

I know of no better illustration of this than the two men matched in a speaking competition before a large crowd of people. Both were to recite the Twenty-third Psalm. The first man was a distinguished-looking, noted orator. His resonant voice rose and fell with the power of ocean waves as it carried to the farthest gallery. When finished, the hall thundered with applause. When the clapping finally died down, the other man stood up. Older, and rather nondescript looking, with graying hair, he was unknown to the crowd. And when he began to speak his words were a bit quavery. However, as the audience strained to listen, the room became completely still. Though his voice was neither deep nor resonant, his offering of the familiar words touched the innermost spirits of those in the hall, giving them a sense of peace, strength, and assurance. When he finished there was no applause, for the people were wiping their eyes. In the awed stillness, the first speaker stepped out on the stage and addressed the audience.

"Ladies and gentlemen," he said quietly, "there is no doubt who was the more effective speaker. The reason is quite clear. Though I can boast that I know every nuance of the Twenty-third Psalm, it is clear to all of us that my worthy colleague knows the Shepherd."

Summing Up

The Principle of Speaking With Authority

1. Concentrate on your message. Don't be thinking of something else.

2. Let your voice reflect your concern, but don't be bombastic or overbearing.

3. Speak from your experience.

4. Speak with the best interest of others at heart.

5. Speak in honesty and love. Double-talk and gloss-overs only lose your listener's respect.

6. Speak as a servant. "Whoever wants to be great must be your servant . . ." said Jesus.

7. Remember the Source of all authority.

—14—
The Principle of Family First

Have you been in this spot?

The older man leaned back in his swivel chair, lit a cigarette, then swung toward the younger man seated across from his desk and exhaled a blue cloud of smoke.

"So you think your overtime is interfering with your family life, eh?" he barked.

The younger man shifted in his chair. "Yes," he said, "particularly when it means working three and four nights a week. I don't mind a night or two, but—"

"If it takes four nights a week to get your job done, then that's what it takes," interrupted the department director.

"But I haven't been able to take my son to his monthly Cub Scout pack meeting since last fall," replied the younger man, "and my wife feels that—"

"Listen, my boy," interjected the boss. "You are absolutely right in being concerned for your family. That's as it should be. But let me tell you something." He put his cigarette down in the ashtray and leaned across the desk. "If you love your family, then your job comes first."

In answer to the young man's quizzical look, he continued. "No doubt about it. Why? Because without your job, how could you support your family? How would they eat? Keep warm in winter?

"So," he added, leaning back in his chair with an air of finality, "if you love your family, then you'll put your work first."

The above scene, which involved a close friend and his department head, took place in a midwestern city some years ago. However, the manager's argument as to which is more important—one's family or job—typifies an attitude still fairly common in some business areas today.

In simple truth, the argument stinks.

It stinks because it reverses the divine order: After God, the family is of first importance. Not only theologians but most anthropologists, sociologists, and psychologists as well, agree. For it is generally held that the strength of a society rests on the solidarity of the family.

Proof can be found in any newspaper. Most of society's misfits and troublemakers come from broken families where there is no real parental authority.

"But being away from home because of your work certainly doesn't mean a 'broken family'," my friend's old boss would argue. In fact, he would be able to point out that a large number of "successful" executives spend much time away from their wives and children. He could very well have pointed to me in this respect.

Cross-Country Family

Not only was I out of town on business trips most of the time but I also moved my family twenty-three times in the first twenty-one years of our marriage. My oldest daughter, Melody, had moved twenty-one times before she was eighteen years old. And she suffered for it. Each time we moved she found herself the new kid on the block. Continually forced to make new friends, she became very insecure. A beautiful girl on the outside, gregarious and seemingly able to talk to anyone, she was lonely and despondent on the inside.

All of these moves were made before I knew anything about the divine order for the family. Interested more in my own job progress than the welfare of my family, I moved my wife and children to various parts of the country without any thought for their well-being. Two of my daughters, Bonnie and Merrilee, were in high school when we moved from Connecticut to Atlanta. As it was during midterm, they could not get the courses they wanted. I sat with them in the school principal's office—both of them were in tears. As I tried to console them, I sensed somewhere deep within me the fact that I was the one responsible for their grief, and yet my ego would not allow me to admit it.

Some years later my daughters went through the same turmoil when we moved back to Connecticut. By this time they had become acclimated to the south, and just when they were beginning to feel at home there, I pulled the rug from under them again.

If I had known then what I know now, we wouldn't have made so many moves. Happily, the situation in the business world has changed for the better. Not only are family men and women taking a second look at promotion opportunities involving a move but corporations are realizing that a happy, stable family makes for a better executive. In addition, the tremendous relocation costs faced by the companies in the sale and purchase of employees' homes and moving expenses are forcing firms to think long and hard about personnel transfers.

Thus it comes down to priorities. Many men and women are giving up their egos and their opportunities for material success, and are putting the good of their families at the top of their priority list. And yet, in the long run, they gain immeasurably more by doing it. Why? Because I believe God created families; He does not put together corporations, committees, or industrial programs. And in creating the family I am sure that He had in mind roles for each of us. The father has his function, the mother hers. And when one doesn't fulfill his role, the family suffers.

Who Does What?

Yes, a husband and wife assume specific roles. But I am not about to get into an argument about who should do what. That's covered enough by groups discussing everything from the pros and cons of women's liberation to the proper functions of a "househusband."

Frankly, I believe that all of the arguments are answered by the Apostle Paul in Ephesians 5:21: "Submit to one another. . . ."

Submit to one another means put the other person's good above your own. To me, that is the whole ball of wax. If two people love each other and want to face the world together, then there is no better way to overcome problems and find their way through the maze than to surrender one to the other.

Unfortunately, too many men ignore verse 21 and focus on the following one: "Wives, submit to your husbands. . . ." Then, they stop reading before reaching verse 28: "Even so, husbands should love their wives as their own bodies," meaning that her wishes are as important as his own. Submitting to each other means family counseling together, frank and open talks with give-and-take around the table with everyone participating.

This involves taking criticism, also. Too often men, who consider themselves the breadwinners, are not inclined to take criticism, especially from their wives. Thus they often pass up valuable guidance. Women seem to have a spirit of discernment, more so than men. And if a wife has strong feelings about a family move, a husband had better seriously consider them.

The Healing Power of Listening

This involves *listening*. And in family meetings where everyone is willing to listen to the group, and to God, much of the benefit arises from that strong sense of communication in which the participants listen to one another.

I saw this work out in an English family who moved to the United States. This was a situation in which the father felt a definite leading to start life anew in America. Though he had no job prospects here, his sense of guidance was so strong that he could not dismiss it as a whim—nor was it a vague hunger for new horizons. So he, his wife, and their two children knelt together in prayer and asked for guidance. Then, following long discussion, the four came to a common agreement that the move was right. The father sold his business, their home, and, with no other sustenance than the deep conviction that they were moving under heavenly guidance, traveled to the United States. When I met them I was struck by a deep sense of peace among the members of the family. And, as it turned out, it was a good move; the father found a promising position in his line of work, they purchased a house, and the children rapidly acclimated to their new homeland.

My English friends' experience illustrates those instances where a relocation may well be in the best interests of everyone involved. Again, this becomes apparent after the family sits down together. If, after discussing all possibilities, they sense that a move is in accord with God's will, then there is nothing for a family to do but step out in faith.

Often, a compromise can be reached. But again, this can only be done when everyone involved is in agreement. A close friend who lived in an urban area was offered a job in another state. It meant living in a rural community 150 miles away. He prayed about it, only, as he admitted to me later, it was a one-sided prayer, in effect: "I want this job." Though he took his wife into full account, he left out one important person: a son at home who was a high school junior. He did not ask his son's opinion about the move, or even discuss it with him.

The move was disastrous for the son; in transferring to a rural school system in the middle of the year, he was unable to acclimate or assimilate into his strange new surroundings. He went on to graduate but had no warm high school memories most students carry with them through life.

"If only I had considered his situation and his feelings," mourned the father. "I could easily have let him remain in his school for his final year and a half by not moving the family so quickly." He went on to say that it would have meant giving up some of his own comfort and convenience, but for the sake of his son it would have been well worth it.

A move under the right conditions can be a real plus for family growth. I know an executive with a nationwide chain of stores who had quite a number of advancements in his extensive career which involved long-distance relocating.

"We were a together family," he says, "with a strong faith support. Instead of fracturing our relationships, our moves welded all of us together into a unit which seemed to get stronger with each transfer.

"Moving was an adventure, with new areas to explore, and new friends to get to know," he adds, "but we couldn't have done it without a strong belief that we had put everything into the hands of God."

There are always those times when a job relocation is in order. And if the decision is reached with total family involvement, the move can be advantageous for everyone concerned.

In my case, this did not happen. Yes, we did have "family counsel" before our moves, but instead of an open forum, the meeting was more my *selling* the family on what I had already planned to do. Instead of putting God and my family first, my own ego held sway.

The Man Who Said No

A shining example of the reverse of this is Matthew Redden, who was regional vice-president of a large insurance company when he faced his crossroads. It happened while he and his family were living in Los Angeles. He was invited to move to the New York office to become a vice-president.

He did what I should have done in my many moves.

He obviously contacted the One who was in charge of his life, then carefully considered his family situation, which involved children in school. Fully realizing that he could well be giving up his only opportunity for advancement, he told the home office no.

Executives usually believe that once one turns down a transfer involving an advancement, he can forget about future promotions.

It was not so with Matthew Redden and his firm. After his children finished school, he was advanced to a vice-presidency in a position much better suited to his talents than the previously offered post he had turned down.

Yes, with God, opportunity does knock more than once.

As almost anyone my age will attest to, the passage of time accelerates with every year. Too often and too late we look back and mourn, "If only. . . ."

When I was a young father, a wise old friend said, "Lee, do you realize that when your children are nine years old, their life with you will be half over?"

I stared at him in shocked disbelief.

"Yes," he sighed, "I can tell you from my own experience. When they're eighteen, they're off to college and from then on. . . ." The poignant look in his eyes told me all that I needed to know.

That's why I like a certain poem written by Dr. Denis Waitley, an authority on human relationships. It's one we should all read and remember when we begin to forget why we are on this earth.

> *There is an Island fantasy*
> *A "Someday I'll" we'll never see*
> *When recession stops, inflation ceases*
> *Our mortgage is paid, our pay increases*
> *That Someday I'll where problems end*
> *Where every piece of mail is from a friend*
> *Where the children are sweet and already grown*
> *Where all the other nations can go it alone*
> *Where we all retire at forty-one*
> *Playing backgammon in the island sun*
> *Most unhappy people look to tomorrow*
> *To erase this day's hardship and sorrow*
> *They put happiness on "layaway"*
> *And struggle through a blue today*
> *But happiness cannot be sought*
> *It can't be earned, it can't be bought*
> *Life's most important revelation*
> *Is that the journey means more than the destination*
> *Happiness is where you are right now*
> *Pushing a pencil or pushing a plow*
> *Going to school or standing in line*
> *Watching and waiting, or tasting the wine*
> *If you live in the past you become senile*
> *If you live in the future you're on Someday I'll*
> *The fear of results is procrastination*
> *The joy of today is a celebration*
> *You can save, you can slave, trudging mile after mile*

But you'll never set foot on your Someday I'll
When you've paid all your dues and put in your time
Out of nowhere comes another Mt. Everest to climb
From this day forward make it your vow
Take Someday I'll and make it your Now![1]

Summing Up

The Principle of Family First

1. Remember the divine order: God, family, you.

2. Consider your family's welfare first before making your plans, whether they involve career, vacation, or other activities.

3. As a husband, are you submissive to your wife (preferring the other above yourself)?

4. As a wife, are you submissive to your husband (preferring the other above yourself)?

5. Do you *listen* to everyone in your family—his or her needs, hopes, ambitions?

6. Will you sacrifice yourself for the family's benefit?

7. Do you place your family's welfare above your own ambitions?

—15—
The Principle of Using Your Talents

Not long after I was discharged from the United States Navy in 1946, I found myself undergoing a peculiar kind of torture. Newly married, with plans to continue college in the fall, I had to find work through the summer to support my wife and myself. Flint, Michigan, was the home of the Buick auto-assembly plant, so I applied there.

I was put to work on the assembly line. My job was to install the window regulators inside the car doors. These were mechanical guides that helped insure the smooth raising and lowering of the car windows.

To install the regulators, I'd walk down the line with an electric bolt-tightening gun over my shoulder as the car bodies, doors open, slowly moved toward me.

I would slip the regulator up through a hole on the left side of the door interior with one hand, start the four bolts with the other, and then drive them home with the automatic tightener.

Each installation was supposed to take thirty seconds. It took me a full minute to install my first one. Challenged, I endeavored to do better with each unit. Within two hours I was able to complete the job in eleven seconds. It was logistically impossible to do it any quicker. From then on, the job became torture as I worked hour after hour, fastening the same four bolts. By the end of the first week I would have done anything to not have to go back. But we had to eat, pay rent, and buy clothing. So, if you have ever purchased a 1946 Buick, there's a good chance that I installed its window regulators.

It was during this time that I learned something about one's calling in life. For I could see that most of my fellow workers were at peace with their jobs. Some had been on the assembly line for ten years and had absolutely no trouble with it. They were suited for it. When our shift ended at four o'clock, they could walk out the door, leave everything behind them, and concentrate on relaxing, whether it was fishing or building rock gardens in their backyards. In no way did they want any job responsibility hanging over their heads after work.

That summer I came to know these men well, and for the most part found them to be well-rounded, good people. Most were superior to me in mechanical skills and some knew more about the world from the standpoint of politics and current events.

My calling lay in a different direction. I loved competition, with myself and with others. I had a sales talent and also liked to read and do research. Put these aptitudes together, and you have an insurance man.

By the same token most of the regular assembly-line workers would probably find selling insurance a bore. I talked to one who had tried it. One day at lunch I asked what he did before working at Buick. He unscrewed the cap of his Thermos and poured a cup of steaming coffee. "Oh, lots of things—clerking in a store, some office work, even sold life insurance." At the mention of the latter, he winced and shook his head. "That insurance job was the worst. After a few months of it I was ready to go out of my mind."

He sipped his coffee and glanced over his shoulder toward the assembly line. "Now, *this* kind of work I like. I feel good at the end of the day, like I've really accomplished something. And whenever I see a Buick go down the street, I take a little credit for its being there."

As I think back on that conversation, I am thankful that each of us has been given a unique talent that enables us to serve others in a special way. Otherwise autos wouldn't be built, insurance wouldn't be sold, and innumerable other needs wouldn't be met to keep this old globe turning.

What is *your* gift?

You have one, or you wouldn't be here. Just as each individual's fingerprint is one of a kind, as each snowflake is geometrically unique, so is each of us gifted with special talents in serving others.

You may be blessed with an artistic talent, a genius for organizing people, an aptitude for salesmanship, a mechanical skill, a bent for research, or the insight of a homemaker.

You may already be employing your special talent in your job, or enjoying it through a hobby, community service activity, or in free-lance assignments after working hours.

Yet, you may also be like so many who mourn, "Oh, I'm not good at anything. I'm lucky to have a job and to be able to plod through it every day."

What an unfortunate misconception.

All you have to do is think back to your youth; what were you particularly good at then? For example, back in seventh or eighth grade, in what subject did you get your best grades? What activity did you particularly enjoy? Were you adept at writing themes and essays? Did math come easy? Was art class a time to which you looked forward? Did biology and other natural sciences intrigue you? Were you anxious for shop class time so you could finish that bookcase or table, or assemble the auto transmission?

Your answers provide clues to your career potential. We tend to excel in what we most enjoy doing.

Unfortunately, as we move on in life, we too often forget this truth as we succumb to the blandishments of glamorous professions, the lure of high-salaried possibilities, or we may simply be swayed by poor advice. Thus too many of us end up living lives as described by philosopher Henry Thoreau, of "quiet desperation."

Today, fortunately, most high schools and colleges have competent counseling services. There are also many career guidance services available—some commercial, some nonprofit. Some are excellent and, sadly, some are little more than high-priced employment agencies. One of the best ways to check these out is to talk with people who have already dealt with them.

Tragically, some of the worst career guidance can come from misguided parents. Too often young people are channeled into professions for which they are not suited, by parents who have not learned to let go of their children. Many of the "flower children" of the sixties who became rootless wanderers were former college students on their way to becoming doctors, lawyers, and other professionals. Chafing under parental pressures to "prepare for a career in which you can become wealthy," they fought back by disdaining all ambitions. Fortunately, many of them later returned to their studies.

Sometimes parental pressure can be exerted very subtly. Almost from the day he was born, Larry's parents had his life all mapped out. Of course he would become a physician like his father. As Larry grew, his mother and father took little note that everything he enjoyed doing, all his interests, pointed to an engineering career. Fascinated with engines, he devised and built miniature factories while other boys struggled with crude model airplanes.

His parents chose not to recognize his interests and when Larry entered high school he was given to understand that this was a first step toward premed studies. Under strong parental authority, Larry finally became a physician, just like his father. Though he was adequate in his profession, he never really enjoyed it, nor did he become very successful at it. Sadly, he died of a heart ailment in his forties.

Should Larry have changed professions in his later years? It's difficult to say how it all would have worked out. But I know of many cases in which such a change worked out for the better.

Changing Careers in Midstream

Two such changes that I read of involved in each case a stockbroker who went out of business during the market recession of the late seventies. One of them had been a fervent cycling enthusiast, so he put his hobby to work. He opened a shop to sell and repair bicycles. Fortunately, this was a time when more and more people were getting into cycling, so his shop became quite a success. When the stock market rebounded, someone asked him if he planned to return to the brokerage business.

He looked up from a bicycle he was repairing, his eyes shining, and said, "And give up all this fun?"

The other broker who had been drastically affected by the recession had always dreamed of opening a country inn—probably when he retired. He was able to borrow money to add to his own savings in order to purchase an inn that was available for a bargain price in New England. "Thank God for that recession," he says today. "I didn't have to wait until I retired to begin having the time of my life!"

But beware of greener grass.

The danger in contemplating a career change is envisioning something that isn't there. This is especially true in midlife when many tend to become jaundiced with their work. The two stockbrokers were forced into finding new careers. They had no illusions of what lay ahead; they knew that it would require dedication and hard work.

Too often men and women in their middle years begin to look at the other side of the fence and see nothing but green when, in fact, it is very weedy.

Discovery at Sea

A man who discovered this early in life was Edward Carlson, who, many years ago, as a young man in Seattle, worked as a bellhop while studying at the University of Washington. He helped support his mother and sister. After two hard years of work and study, it all got to him.

One beautiful spring day when the other students were talking about taking girls canoeing and playing tennis, he walked to the window in the school library and stared gloomily at the Seattle skyline.

The only girls he would be seeing were those for whom he lugged suitcases in the Camlin Hotel in downtown Seattle, where he worked every night from 11:00 P.M. to 7:00 A.M. During the day he cracked the books to cram for his second-year finals. Classes from 8:00 A.M. to noon didn't leave much time for anything else.

Standing there at the window he wondered, *Why waste my best years working and studying like this?* Beyond the Seattle buildings he could envision blue Puget Sound curving out into the Pacific mist. Somewhere steaming into that mist would be a black-hulled liner, her white superstructure glinting in the sun.

Two days later he was at the seamen's hall getting his shipping papers. He signed on as an ordinary seaman on the SS *President Lincoln,* bound for Yokohama, Japan.

Three days later he was at sea, and the fresh ocean breeze in his face convinced him even more that he was free. After he spent the first few days swabbing decks and chipping rust, an officer discovered he could type. So he became a yeoman and secretary to the captain and first mate. As he filed reports and typed letters, he watched the ship's officers at work.

"I began to notice a certain quality about them," he said. "Everybody had a job to do and he did it, day in, day out. There was no special excitement about it, no glamour. If anything, there was a certain quiet pride these men took in working together to meet daily goals, come good weather or bad.

"It all came home to me one night," he continued, "as I stood at the rail watching the moon rise above the dark waters. I could hear the sighing hiss of the bow wave and the low rhythmic thumping of the ship's engines.Those engines never faltered,hour after hour. They would cross five thousand miles of ocean.

"There was a certain resoluteness about it all," he said, "the engines, the men. A harmony of perseverance. A harmony in tune with the dynamic pulse of the universe God set in motion eons ago."

And that's when Edward Carlson decided to return to his hotel job and university studies. From bellhop, Edward worked his way up to president of Western International Hotels. In December of 1970, at the age of fifty-nine, he was named president of United Airlines. The line was in financial trouble at the time.

However, he began a campaign to turn it around, to raise employee morale and develop efficiency throughout the company. He traveled daily along the line's network of cities, turning up in hangars and sales offices, meeting baggage handlers and mechanics, chatting with stewardesses and pilots. Within a year United was back in the black.

"That lesson I learned aboard ship helped me get through some rough times," he said. "And it's one I try to pass on to others. For we all continually face gritty responsibilities one way or another, in our jobs or at home. And sometimes they seem to be interminable.

"I know the temptation is always there to take the easy way out. A fair horizon always beckons. But the Bible says, 'No one who puts his hand to the plow and looks back is fit for the kingdom of God.'[1]

"If we take the easy way out, we break the beat God has set for our life. But if we face our responsibilities directly, He will always give us the help we need.

"Often it's tough to keep plowing that furrow and not look back. But it's that furrow that's going to lead us to the success He has planned for us."

As we can see, Edward Carlson's true calling was management. And that lonely night aboard the ship plying the Pacific waters was when he finally realized it.

Summing Up

The Principle of Using Your Talents

1. You're on your way when you discover your gift or talent.

2. Are you putting your talent to good use?

3. It's never too late to change occupations *if* there is good reason for it.

4. Be alert to direction from your power source.

5. Good counseling from experts is vital.

6. Do not let yourself be sidetracked through worldly circumstances.

7. Beware of parental pressure, for both your own and your children's sake.

8. Remember that the greener grass on the other side of the fence may be just a good bed of weeds.

9. Perseverance in your work brings its own reward.

—16—
The Principle of Surrender

You probably had the same problem I had when I was a boy.

The white canvas bag hung over the back of a chair in our kitchen in Flint like a mournful reproach. I was nine years old and for three days I had steered clear of it, feeling guilty every time I saw it. For the bag signified *getting started*.

The bag had SATURDAY EVENING POST emblazoned on it and represented my first job. Three days earlier I was supposed to have started selling copies of this magazine door-to-door. It would be a vital enterprise, for the profit from each five-cent sale would help put food on a very bare table for my mother, my younger brother, and me.

I had never sold anything before, and the very thought of walking up to someone and asking him or her to *buy* something terrified me.

I pictured all sorts of diabolical things happening: a housewife screaming at me to stop bothering her—vicious dogs leaping at me from behind front-walk bushes—even someone calling the police.

Though I was too young to realize the true nature of my concern, the gulf between that canvas bag of magazines and me was fear—fear of rejection, fear of failure.

Finally, on the fourth day, my mother let me know in no uncertain terms that after school that afternoon I would begin working my route. After all, she reminded me, I had made a promise to the man at the distribution agency.

Surrendering to my mother was easy, especially when she had that look in her eye. After my father died, she had to take on the role of both parents, and that meant administering corporal punishment. The word *corporal* comes from the Latin word meaning "body" and that is where she would administer it, on the lower, rear part.

And so I surrendered to the reality that I had better get myself out on the street and sell magazines.

An icy November wind knifed through me as I stood on the sidewalk, the canvas bag slung over my shoulder. *Which house first?* I wondered. Not the one next door, where the family kept a large dog, I decided. Nor the one next to it, where the neighborhood grouch lived; she would call the police for sure.

As I stood there on the windswept street I *knew* I couldn't sell anything. I was certain of it. I looked back at our house. The light was on and a shadow moved across the window. I knew it was my mother. I also knew what she would do if I returned, admitting I hadn't tried.

Taking a deep breath, I headed to the house directly across the street. I did not know the family. I will never forget those gray-painted wooden steps leading up to that foreboding door. Slowly I climbed them, the loose dime-store rubber sole on my right shoe catching on each step. Finally, I faced the door. Next to it glared a bell button.

Tentatively, I extended a finger. Swallowing hard, I pressed the bell, fervently hoping that no one was home. Dimly, within the interior, I heard a sound. I waited, new flakes of snow settling on a ragged coat sleeve. Then the door curtains were pulled back and a figure loomed behind the glass.

My throat felt frozen; I couldn't talk. I held up a copy of the magazine with its Norman Rockwell cover.

"What do you want?" a muffled voice demanded.

"Er, uh," I stammered, "you wouldn't want to buy a copy of the *Saturday Evening Post,* would you?"

The figure muttered something, the curtain fluttered back into place, and the steps receded away from the door.

It seemed awfully quiet on that lonely street. Snow was softly rounding off the steps on which I stood, and the streetlights shed yellow pools of light on the sidewalk.

But something important had taken place: I had made my first sales call.

The worst that could have happened had happened: I had been rejected. But I had not suffered as I feared. The fact that someone did not want a copy of the magazine seemed no earthshaking disaster.

My stepping up to that first door had demolished a barrier: fear. Fear of failure.

Now that I had faced it, it had lost its power to intimidate me. I walked down the steps and headed for the next house, a new confidence in me. That person didn't buy, either, but the one at the third house did. And I returned home that evening feeling like a conquering hero. I had sold all my inventory. It marked the beginning of my sales career.

Finding Freedom From Fear

Fear of failure is probably one of the most prevalent and insidious blocks anyone faces in getting started on any worthwhile project. Note the word *worthwhile.* No adult seems to have trouble with small tasks such as mowing the lawn, washing the car, or carrying out the garbage. Who ever worried about doing a great job with the garbage?

But give a person the task of preparing a new sales campaign, planning the program for a church group, or selling magazines from door to door for the first time, and you will often find that person caught in the trap: fear of failure.

It is this same fear that holds back a young man from asking a girl to go out with him because he feels sure she will turn him down.

And what suffers if we fail? Our ego, that grand picture our mind paints of us standing victorious on that pedestal of *success*. We shrink from starting anything that might damage it. The fact is that picture does not really exist.

To venture out you must first

Surrender Ego

Throw yourself into the assignment or project without worrying whether or not you'll succeed. Surrender yourself to getting the job done.

An outstanding cavalry commander was the Civil War General Philip Sheridan, who accomplished many seemingly impossible battlefield victories. When asked his secret of success, he answered, "I never give counsel to my fears."

When I started that first *Saturday Evening Post* sales trip, I knew very little about the power of Jesus Christ, but I had learned something about the surrender principle. For, in calling on that first prospect, I had surrendered my fear of failure to a higher motivation, a resolute mother, and the knowledge that my effort would help put food on my family's table.

Today, I still face assignments and projects that make me tremble. In the fall of 1983, I had a five-bypass open-heart operation, a fearsome experience, believe me. As a result, I surrendered all my natural fears to the One who told us, "Trust in the Lord with all thine heart; and lean not unto thine own understanding."[1]

Once you make that first move, you overcome a powerful barrier. It happens when you

Surrender the Preconception

For years aeronautical scientists believed that airplanes would have difficulty breaking the sound barrier. Their belief, based on scientific theory and limited experiments, held that the aircraft would break apart at the speed at which sound travels, about 700 miles per hour at flight levels at that time, for it would collide with its own sound waves and disintegrate. The speed of sound varies from 762 miles per hour at higher altitudes up to 82,000 feet, after which it increases.

Despite this, attempts to break the sound barrier were made, and planes did crash. Finally, on October 14, 1947, Chuck Yeager, a United States Air Force test pilot, flew a specially designed plane over nine hundred miles per hour. He reported some initial buffeting but all went well, opening the way for commercial intercontinental flight today at supersonic speeds.

How often have I heard the claims that "you can never sell insurance in that area," or "that association will never buy group insurance; we have tried to sell to it for years."

The answer is to study the problem. Just as aeronautical engineers finally developed an aircraft that would maintain its integrity when passing through the sound barrier, so did we investigate the group insurance business and found that many organizations were good prospects when shown how they could be helped.

But one must surrender the preconceived belief that it can't be done. Then one's talents and ingenuity are released to work on the problem without hindrance.

Take the case of Harry Houdini and the mysterious door. The famous magician was challenged to open a door fitted with an elaborate vault-type lock. He went at it, confident that he would open it in seconds or minutes at the most. But after twenty minutes, he was still hard at work, his brow furrowed in perplexity. For an entire hour he struggled with the lock, but it still resisted his efforts. Finally, after such a long period of concentrated effort, Houdini slumped against the door in frustration. It swung open. It had never been locked! But in Houdini's mind it had been locked and for all practical purposes, it was.

Surrender your preconception that "the door is locked," that "it can't be done." Preconceptions are usually misconceptions.

Preconceptions cause detours, yes, but something far more insidious that can delay your start is a malady described by a word coming from two Latin words meaning "of tomorrow." The word? *Procrastination.*

Surrender Those Tomorrows

It is all too human to think we "own" our tomorrows, that we can always call the shots. Sad as it may seem, sometimes our tomorrows never come and until we surrender our dependence on them we fall prey to procrastination.

Some years ago a writer friend I'll call Zach began talking about doing a book on George Washington Carver, the famed scientist who, by finding countless uses for the peanut, helped rejuvenate the economy of southern agriculture, once totally dependent on cotton. Zach waxed enthusiastic about the fascinating information he had discovered in his research about Carver. He had prepared an outline for his book but somehow never sat down to write it. Whenever I asked him how it was going, his eyes would brighten and he'd reply, "Great, I'm starting on it right away." Or, "Don't expect to see much of me after next week because that's when I'm really going to get cracking on it."

"Right away" never seemed to come. And then, about two years later, I opened my Sunday newspaper book section to find a review hailing a new book on George Washington Carver—by another author.

Zach might as well forget his book. It seems that in the grand scheme of things, if someone doesn't follow up on a good idea, another person will develop it.

All too often I have heard good ideas expounded at luncheon tables and then, when not acted upon, turn up in another company where they have been put to good use.

It is good that *someone* is there to take advantage of a good idea. The tragic side of this, however, is when a good idea that could benefit the human race is not acted upon. How many scientists before Jonas Salk came along, I wonder, were on the verge of discovering a polio vaccine, only to fall prey to some form of delay? How many lives would have been saved if they had diligently followed up their leads?

"There's Plenty of Time"

That is why I believe there is a diabolical element in human affairs which engenders procrastination. Some simply call it an inner wish to postpone something one doesn't wish to do; others term it a numbing spiritual sickness. I call it a devilish delaying tactic. Yes, I believe in a devil, a spirit of evil with an aim of beguiling humans away from doing good. One of his ploys is to whisper in his victim's ear, "There's plenty of time." It happens when a free-lance writer sharpens pencils instead of sitting down at his typewriter, when a housewife turns on the television instead of cleaning her living room, when a student goes out for a hamburger instead of studying for that final exam.

All of them duck the truth that there is *not* plenty of time. The writer never finishes his article, the housewife is too embarrassed to invite guests in, and the student fails his exam.

The best defense I know against procrastination is to do the job right now. But of course this isn't always possible. The next best thing is to set up an appointment time for the task and stick to it. The writer determines a work schedule from 9:00 A.M. to 3:00 P.M. every day; the housewife promises to get the dusting done before "General Hospital" comes on the air, and the student determines that by midnight Saturday he will have completed his studying.

"Sure," someone will respond, "but I have difficulty keeping on a schedule."

Set a Deadline for Yourself

Here's a surefire remedy: Commit yourself to an unbreakable deadline which, if broken, will prove embarrassing to you.

Richard had been "meaning to" redecorate his family's living room for months. Somehow he could never get around to it. One day his wife had an idea. "Richard," she said, "let's invite our friends over for a party and tell them it's an occasion to debut our 'new' living room—three weeks from now."

Richard thought it was an excellent idea, and with this incentive had the room completed in plenty of time.

A friend in the insurance business, when given an assignment, always works out a reasonable deadline with his department head, even though no actual due date for the job has been set. However, he knows that a real deadline nipping at his heels will inspire him to finish the job on time.

When DeWitt Wallace, founder of the *Reader's Digest,* put together his first issue, he sat in the New York Public Library writing condensations of magazine articles he planned to use. With a publishing deadline in mind, he committed himself to a goal of condensing one article per day. Some days found him working furiously right up to closing time, but he kept to his schedule, and founded a publishing empire.

There is a dynamic principle in this kind of commitment which you can put to work on your behalf when you

Surrender Yourself

A veteran track coach, in guiding athletes who were out to break the high-jump record, told them, "Throw your heart over the bar and the rest of you will follow."

When a person completely dedicates himself to a project, it's on its way to being completed. And dedicating oneself often means taking that first step.

Take my friend Dick, for example. After moving into a new home, he and his wife found one drawback to it. The backyard was an uninviting, dank square of ground. "Wouldn't it be nice to make it into a brick patio with a rock garden surrounding it?" suggested his wife.

"Yes," agreed Dick, "with a recirculating fountain in that higher corner over there." I later learned that he had always dreamed of having such a fountain.

However, two years passed and nothing was done about it. Dick planned to do it "when he had the time," but of course, that never happened. One winter day while shopping at a nearby store, he noticed a closeout section of garden items. There it was—a recirculating fountain being offered at a once-in-a-life-time price. He quickly snapped it up and brought it home, storing it in the garage.

But something dynamic happened with the purchase of that fountain. Dick knew that by spring he had to get the patio started. He took out library books on patio construction, nosed around supply houses for the best price on bricks. By spring he was ready to begin work, and well before the end of summer Dick and his family were enjoying a lovely patio garden.

"But that doesn't always work," argued a friend when I told

him this story. "My wife wanted a rose garden and I bought two dozen rosebushes. I never got around to planting them and one day they were all dead. Where did I miss the boat?"

The difference was easy to see. My friend with the rosebushes was accustomed to buying rather extravagantly. He could afford to; buying two dozen rosebushes was no great commitment on his part. But in Dick's case, buying the fountain was quite an investment, the kind that impelled him to finish the job.

Perhaps if my rose-fancier friend had invested in two dozen expensive, prize-winning varieties, he would have gotten them in the ground in time.

Another example is a New York friend who discovered in the house he bought that the former owner had a window alcove in the master bedroom walled up to form a closet—a closet which my friend thought unnecessary since there were two other closets in the room. For three years he and his wife talked about removing the false wall to open up the alcove and let much-needed light into the room. But it seemed to be such a formidable job that it was never done. The husband talked about asking a carpenter to estimate the project. His wife worried about a long period of construction mess in the bedroom.

One winter the man's brother came for a visit. When he heard about the covered-up alcove, he said, "Let's investigate." The brother was an enthusiastic handyman. He began by boring a small peephole in the wall to determine the type of interior construction. "Simple," he declared, and pulled a large piece of wallboard away.

My friend and his wife gasped. But the die had been cast. There was no turning back. He and his brother went at it with a crowbar and hammer. It turned out to be fairly easy work. Before that evening was over, the entire false wall had been removed, along with the old studding. And the bedroom then contained a beautiful alcove with a window. In the actual doing, it turned out to be a simple job. It was in the couple's fearful imagination that the molehill had grown into a mountain.

Surrender the Mountain

Often when facing a task, we become intimidated by it and find ways to avoid it. The Bible says it this way: "The slothful man saith, There is a lion in the way; a lion is in the streets. As the door turneth upon his hinges, so doth the slothful upon his bed."[2]

Somehow our sloth and our fears magnify the task before us to the point where the mouse darting across the cobblestones becomes a lion in the street. And we're afraid to go outdoors.

When I had my first desk in the insurance business, it would often get away from me. After being on a field trip for several days, I would return to find it stacked high with letters to answer, reports to handle, papers to study. I would be disheartened to the point where I avoided it; quite simply, it had become "a lion in the street"; it intimidated me.

I found myself picking up papers, glancing at them, worrying about how to handle them, and putting them down again. All the while my mind was boggled by the amount of work facing me.

Then a veteran insurance man, long experienced with such desks, gave me a tip.

"Lee," he said, "when you sit down at your desk, sort the papers into two piles: 'urgent' and 'priority.' Then, pick up just one piece of paper from the top of the 'urgent' pile, take care of it, and then go on to the next piece of paper. Don't worry about the stacks; concentrate on the one job at hand. When it is done, pick up another piece of paper and do the same. You'll be surprised how well this works."

I tried it. At first it was difficult not to worry about the stacks looming in front of me. But I steeled myself to picking up that one piece of paper and handling it before going on to the next one. It worked. By concentrating on one job, without letting the stacks intimidate me, I had cleared off my desk before the end of the day.

It's a common problem, staring at the mountain. A friend of my wife had the same difficulty. I discovered it one day when we visited her. I was astonished at her house; it looked as if

Oscar Madison of the Odd Couple lived in it. Dirty dishes were piled in the sink, children's toys were strewn from room to room, clothing to be washed and clothing to be ironed was piled high on chairs.

She was a close friend, otherwise I know she wouldn't have invited us in. She was also a realist and I was intrigued by the sign she had hanging in her kitchen: BLESS THIS MESS.

Caroline apologized. "Even that sign is wrong," she mourned. "I know God doesn't bless messes. But what can I do?" She continued, "I'll start to pick up the toys, then I see the clothes that need ironing, while worrying about the dishes in the sink. Suddenly, it all seems too much for me so I put on my coat, jump into the car, and go shopping. But the house is still waiting for me when I get back," she sighed. "It doesn't go away."

I told her what my friend said about my desk. "Look at one thing, not at the mountain."

The next time we visited Caroline, her house was spick-and-span and she was beaming. "It was simple," she said. "First I concentrated on the dishes, then while they were in the washer, I went after the toys. When those were picked up I got my ironing out of the way.

"You know," she laughed, "before I learned how to handle it, I think I expended more energy just looking at the work than taking care of it."

Norman Vincent Peale has a marvelous illustration of this. When he and his wife would drive up to their summer place they would often arrive at night. A rough path of stepping-stones led from the parking area to the house. On stepping out of the car with a flashlight, he discovered that it would not illuminate the entire path, just the stones directly in front of him. However, by stepping from one stone to another, he could reach the house quite easily.

Members of Alcoholics Anonymous employ this same principle in their rehabilitation. Their well-known success formula "one day at a time" often begins as "one minute at a time." A friend who had successfully gone through the program said that "if I could get through one minute without taking a drink, then I could concentrate on the next one." Eventually he worked up to ten minutes, fifteen, an hour, and then in mastering a day, he began mastering a lifetime.

Successful people surrender the mountain.

I like to think of how the young Hebrew boy, David, went out to meet Goliath. Instead of letting himself become intimidated by the thought of facing the giant, he dealt with the most important thing for the moment. He leaned down to the streambed and chose five smooth stones for his sling. He did not look at the mountain.

With all of the above, there still is the age-old nemesis we all face. It goes by various names: lethargy, lassitude, laziness, or sloth.

Surrender the Sloth

There is a part of our nature that just doesn't want to work. That's why companies make money coming up with "laborsaving" devices such as electric pencil sharpeners, automatic toothbrushes, even electric erasers. It is amazing how we duck work. It all stems, I feel sure, from the day Adam was kicked out of the Garden and told he would have to labor by the sweat of his brow. We have been grousing about it ever since.

How to handle it? I knew one man who stepped up his incentive through fear. "I always worry about not getting my work done," he told me. "I believe that deep-down fear keeps me running." It kept him running all right, running too much. Two years after he told me that, he was gone at age fifty-four from a heart attack.

There are better ways of overcoming sloth. My own method is to pray for help. The Apostle James advised in the New Testament, "Submit yourselves therefore to God. Resist the devil, and he will flee from you."[3]

I have found this works. When I feel reluctant to get going in a job, I force myself to do *something,* anything, as long as it's part of the task. The very *doing* is resisting the devil, or sloth, whatever you may wish to call the problem. And it is not long before it fades, or "flees" from you.

A friend who wanted to write but couldn't seem to get started asked a successful novelist his secret. "It's the application of one's bottom to a chair in front of a typewriter. Then, put something down on paper. If you can't think of an appropriate lead sentence, then put down *anything* pertinent, even if it's just stream-of-consciousness writing. At least that gets you started. And once started, you are on your way."

He was talking about overcoming initial lethargy by action. Once inertia is overcome, a dynamic principle comes into being. It is like moving a freight car. It takes a lot of power to get it started, but once it's rolling it takes much less effort to maintain speed.

And again, remember who you are working for. An ancient prayer I came across regarding sloth has been helpful to me:

> *Defend me, O Lord, against idleness and the misuse of time which can never come back; lest my life be unprofitable to Thee, mischievous to others, and without honor or joy to myself; through Jesus Christ our Lord. Amen.*

About this time someone will say, "Getting started is fine, but getting started in *what?*" This is a good question, especially when jobs are scarce.

Many people complain to me, "I have ambition. I want to do more with my life than what I'm doing. But I feel frustrated not knowing what to do."

To them I have one recommendation:

Surrender to the Need

Again, I use a simple success formula which I picked up from Norman Vincent Peale, a six-word sentence that has launched millions of men and women in successful enterprises: *Find a need and fill it.*

To illustrate, let me tell you about two executives with whom I am familiar; one lived about five thousand years ago in the Middle East and the other one is quite active today. Both followed the six-word formula. One was Nehemiah, executive aide to King

Artaxerxes of Persia who, during his time, was probably closest to being a world ruler, since he headed most of the known countries. He was a good man and sympathetic to the Jews, many of whom lived in Persia. In fact, he had allowed a number of them to return to Jerusalem, where they had already rebuilt the Temple.

Artaxerxes' most trusted administrator was a Jew named Nehemiah, who had already distinguished himself in the royal court. When Nehemiah's brother, who had been living in Jerusalem, returned for a visit, Nehemiah eagerly asked for news about their homeland.

His brother looked at the ground and shook his head. "Not good at all," he mourned. "The walls of the city have never been repaired; the people living in it are poverty-stricken and live in fear of their enemies."

Nehemiah knew that there were tribes outside of Jerusalem who hated the Jews and would stop at nothing to take over the city. He was heartsick and saw the need. But at the time he didn't know how to fill it. He had a responsible job in Artaxerxes' court. And, besides, what could he do for those living so far away in Jerusalem?

However, Nehemiah did the only thing I believe any of us need do when we are in a quandary about a problem and don't know what to do about it. He surrendered himself to God. He fasted and prayed, asking for guidance.

In the meantime, he didn't mope around and let his work slide. On the contrary, he worked especially hard to fulfill his administrative duties.

But no easy answer to his prayer boomed from heaven. God did answer, however, and he replied through King Artaxerxes. As the two discussed a governmental problem one day, Artaxerxes took a long look at his aide and said, in effect, "Nehemiah, you look like you've lost your last shekel. Why so sad?"

At first Nehemiah was afraid to answer. Had his sadness made the king angry? But knowing it pays to speak the truth, he answered with the respectful salutation all men used in those days: "Let the king live forever." And then he said what was on his mind. "I am sad because a once great city, Jerusalem, my home city, lies in ruins."

"And what do you want to do about it?" asked the king.

Nehemiah's heart lifted. But before he answered, he surrendered his will to God, asking Him to help him come up with the right answer. Then he spoke: "If it meets your approval, and I have proven valuable to you, then all I request is that you send me to Jerusalem so I can rebuild the city of my fathers."

After considering this, the king asked, "How long will it take you?"

It was a vital question, and it would have been tempting for Nehemiah to give the king a pleasing though unrealistic answer.

A few salesmen have been known to give such answers, telling a buyer that his order will be delivered shortly while knowing full well that the factory is behind on shipments.

But Nehemiah had surrendered his will and, come what may, could only tell the truth. Looking levelly at his boss he said, "It will take a long, long time to make that trip and rebuild all the walls."

Being frank and candid had an interesting effect on Nehemiah. It stimulated his courage and he was given a deep assurance.

"Oh, king," he continued, "if it pleases you, give me official letters of introduction to the governors of the territories I'll pass through to help me on my journey." Quickly thinking further, he added, "And give me a letter to the head of your forestry department asking him to supply us with wood for the work."

There is a right time to ask for favors and Nehemiah knew this was it. Obviously, the king was impressed by his candor and forthrightness. For not only did the king agree to Nehemiah's requests but he did more: He sent an army contingent along with Nehemiah and his staff, which proved to be a boon for them. The heads of the territories through which Nehemiah had to pass hated the folks in Jerusalem and the last thing they wanted was to see the city fortified. But because of the credentials the king supplied to Nehemiah, the territorial leaders were forced to let him pass.

Finally, he reached Jerusalem. After taking time for only a

brief rest, he surveyed the work to be done, riding his horse among the rubble of the walls. Then he held a staff meeting with city leaders, telling them why he was there and letting them know that God had made it all possible. Inspired, they answered with one voice, "Let's get the job done!"

Work started immediately, with every able-bodied man and woman clearing out rubble. Each family was given its own section of the wall on which to work—an early example of allocation of responsibility in giving them the same sense of participation which inspires Japanese workers in setting outstanding records today.

In the meantime, Nehemiah worked right along with his people, chipping stones, moving the heavy blocks, helping build the wall. This spurred the people to greater efforts. When Jerusalem's enemies saw the progress being made, they did everything to sabotage it by attempting to spread discord among the workers.

But the enthusiastic, happy wall builders weren't susceptible to such sabotage and they went right on working, not even bothering to answer their detractors. This only made the enemy angrier and they planned an attack. However, suspecting this, Nehemiah supplied each worker with a sword along with a stone hammer and when the enemy saw everyone working on the wall with a tool in one hand and a weapon in the other, they got cold feet.

In an unbelievable fifty-two days, the walls were finished. Jerusalem had become a real city again.[4]

There are many businessmen like Nehemiah living today, men who use his same basic principles.

The Ferrucci Principle

One of these men is Peter Ferrucci. When he had reached age forty-two, he felt blocked by his company affiliation. After spending his life in the investment business, he felt he had not accomplished all that he could for his clients.

However, instead of moping around, or going through the noted "midlife crisis," he applied the old six-word formula: *Find a need and fill it.*

During his years in the investment business, Ferrucci's clients had often asked him questions about financial matters other than investments. "How do we go about buying a house?" they would ask. "What about paying for our children's education?" "What do we do about reducing our taxes?" "How do we plan our budget? Insurance? Bank accounts? Our estate?"

People were confused. Who could be trusted for honest and objective financial counsel?

Peter Ferrucci saw a need and decided to fill it.

How would he do it? He wondered. Work with an established insurance company? A brokerage house? Start a company?

First came a lot of prayer and seeking of God's guidance. Ferrucci decided to begin a financial consulting practice. But first he made the Lord Chairman of the Board. He rented office space and hired a secretary and an accountant to help him.

Then he "got up on the wall," working with his clients and their problems, teaching them how to find solutions.

Within five years, Peter Ferrucci's firm was an outstanding success, employing fourteen Christian people in helping clients with their financial needs from cash flow to taxes to investments to insurance and real estate.

He had found a need. After committing himself to fill it, and then sharing responsibility and benefits in filling it with others, he fulfilled that client need and also created job opportunities for other Christians.

A Lonely Spot

When I was made responsible for group insurance at New York Life, I found myself thrust into an entirely new field. All my previous experience had been in individual life policies and I knew nothing about selling group insurance. I had no idea of how to contact organizations and associations such as teachers' unions and corporate groups in selling group policies from major medical to disability coverage.

The temptation was to try and bluff it out, pretend I knew more about it than I did. But I also knew that in the end it wouldn't work.

I surrendered my ego and went out into the field, hand in hand with the salesmen, making calls. During the first three years I made 250 sales calls with them. I learned a lot and was also able to pass on some of the techniques and helps I had learned in individual life sales. During that first year, New York Life group insurance annual sales rose from 39 million to 75 million dollars. Within two years we were hitting 100 million dollars a year. It would not have happened if I had not surrendered.

Summing Up

The Principle of Surrender

1. *Surrender Ego:* Never give counsel to your fears.

2. *Surrender the Preconception:* Remember the impassable sound barrier.

3. *Surrender Those Tomorrows:* "There's plenty of time," whispers the enemy.

4. *Surrender Yourself:* Throw your heart over the bar and the rest of you will follow.

5. *Surrender the Mountain:* Do one thing at a time.

6. *Surrender the Sloth:* Do something, anything, as long as it's part of the task.

7. *Surrender to the Need:* Find a need and fill it.

How I Found My Secret Source of Power

Throughout this book I have referred to a "power source," a "higher power." A very real help, it has been a source of inspirational strength which has sustained and invigorated me through trials and crises.

It has given me wisdom far beyond that of my own ability; it has provided guidance and discernment, and, more than anything, it has given me a joy which, in my sixty-second year, fills me with excitement about the future.

This power is available to anyone who longs for it, who believes in it, and who is humble enough to admit that he or she is helpless without it.

Here is how I found it.

Every time I drive by a little stone church in Ridgefield, Connecticut, a mixture of emotions floods me. On one hand I am embarrassed by what I did there one evening. On the other, I feel very grateful.

It happened in 1969 when I was zone vice-president in charge of sales for the eastern half of the United States with the New

York Life Insurance Company. My wife, four children, and I were living in New Canaan, Connecticut, from which I commuted to my Manhattan office. New Canaan marked our thirteenth move to various locations across the country—not too abnormal for an executive on the way up.

My work with New York Life necessitated my being away from home a lot, so it was a little unusual for me to be at home that night. My wife, Audrey, had gone to a Bible study which she had started attending.

When she returned home she came over to my chair, leaned down, kissed me, and said, "Lee, today I accepted Jesus as my Lord and Saviour."

"That's nice," I murmured, buried in my *Wall Street Journal.*

She might as well have said she had had the car washed that day, for all it meant to me, even though we were churchgoers and Audrey and I had led a youth group and taught Sunday school for ten years.

A few weeks later she prevailed upon me to accompany her to a church called Saint Stephen's in Ridgefield. We took two of her friends, and I grudgingly sat with some two hundred other people in the little stone building, listening to an Episcopal priest speak about miracles.

Miracles, I sniffed silently. *I've been a top insurance salesman, have two degrees, and here I sit listening to some nut talk about miracles. What in the world has Audrey gotten herself into?*

Then they had an altar call. This was something new to me— people going forward and kneeling. My curiosity got the better of me and I joined them. As I knelt at the rail a young Thai layman stepped over, placed his hands on my head, and prayed for me.

I didn't like the idea; resentment burned within me. Rising abruptly, I wheeled about and stomped down the aisle toward the door. Stopping next to a white-faced Audrey, who was sitting halfway down the aisle, I barked in a voice the whole congregation could hear, "Audrey, this is a hoax! If you want to stay, okay, but I'm leaving."

I marched outside into the cool night air, planning to wait in

— 212 —

the car. Then I remembered—Audrey had the car keys. My fury kept me warm as I trudged impatiently around the grounds.

"What tripe," I muttered to myself, kicking at leaves. Though I was a churchgoer, my god was hard work. It was the only thing, I believed, that really got one anywhere. Hadn't my life proved it?

When the service ended Audrey came outside and found me. My anger had cooled, but now I was embarrassed.

"Lee," she said, "they're serving coffee and cookies at the rectory. Won't you come?"

"Audrey," I muttered, "all I want to do is go home."

"But we have the other two ladies with us," she said. "You could at least be polite."

"Okay," I grunted.

We walked over to the rector's house and joined the others in the crowded living room. By now I was really embarrassed and tried to blend in with some draperies in a corner.

I wasn't successful. A young girl who had sung at the service that evening came up to talk. She seemed pleasant enough.

"Do you go to this church?" I asked.

"No, I'm Catholic," she replied.

Now I really was confused. What was a Catholic girl doing singing Baptist hymns in an Episcopal church?

Three weeks later, Audrey wanted me to go with her to a Wednesday-evening Bible study at Saint Paul's Episcopal Church in Darien, Connecticut. The rector was Arthur Lane and the study was held in his living room.

Before we left our house, I stopped my wife at the door. "Audrey, if this meeting is a regular, sensible Bible study, okay. But I'm warning you, if it's anything like that last mess, I'm going to get up and leave."

Graciously, she said nothing. When we joined the other people in Art Lane's living room, I was relieved to see that it seemed just like any other study group. Everyone looked normal, although they represented various denominations, including a Catholic nun and a Jew. Even Art Lane seemed like a regular kind of fellow.

But hardly half an hour had passed before I noticed something unusual in that room. Somehow, deep down, I knew that those people loved me.

Anger roiled within. The little boy inside of me, who had been so fearful of poverty and who had felt so rejected, still was insecure despite his material success. I had never experienced unqualified love before.

To hide my feelings, I found myself becoming argumentative. Someone would read a Bible passage and share what it meant to him. Others would agree, and then turn to me.

"Doesn't it speak to you?" one of them asked.

"No, it doesn't," I said, mouth set.

Every once in a while I shot Audrey an "I told you so" look.

That night in the car, driving home, I said, "Those people talk about God as if He's right in their hip pockets."

She was silent.

"I'm not going back next Wednesday," I snorted.

Still she said nothing.

I felt the battle was won, anyway, since I was usually out of town midweek on business. Being home this Wednesday had been unexpected.

But something unusual happened again. For the first time in years I was home again the following Wednesday night—and for seven more Wednesdays. We attended the Bible study every one of those nights.

The seventh Wednesday was a cold December evening; we got out of the car and walked briskly up the walk to the rector's house. Art Lane came to the door to greet us. And then the second most embarrassing thing that happened to me that year took place.

Before Art had a chance to say hello, I burst into tears. I didn't know why I was crying, but I couldn't help it. I stumbled into the foyer and wept.

After slipping into the living room, I sat down in a corner chair and held my Bible in front of my face to hide my tears. Try as I might, I could not stop them. It was as if all the teaching I had heard had finally reached something inside of me, something that was breaking open the cold, hard dam within me.

For three hours that evening I listened as the others discussed Bible passages in an illuminating way I had never heard before. At the end of the evening, as the prayer group softly prayed together, everything finally broke open within me. I found myself kneeling on the rug before them, lifting my hands to heaven and pleading, "Lord Jesus, I guess I'm not much good. But if You want me, I am Yours."

It was as simple as that. All of my former fear, insecurity, and anger was washed away. The little boy of the past had been set free. I was a whole person with Jesus.

The next morning began the first day of a brand-new life for me.

It was especially apparent on the New York subway train which I took to my office every morning from the Grand Central railroad terminal. Usually I detested the ride with what I called the Great Unwashed of New York City. But this morning a warm love filled my heart for each of my fellow passengers—the shopping-bag lady drowsing in the corner, the long-haired youth in grimy jeans, the heavyset man who smelled of garlic.

I loved them all. I knew each one was God's child and that He loved each one and eventually wanted each to be in heaven with Him. I was no different than they were—no better, no worse.

It made quite a difference in my work. Gone was the overbearing, aggressive attitude. I found I was able to see problems more clearly when I looked at them from the other person's viewpoint. Just as with the Apostle Paul, negative aspects were washed away and positive elements emphasized.

I had discovered my secret source of power and His name is Jesus.

I was still ambitious, but now it was directed outward: What will benefit the customer? my fellow employee? the company? These questions became foremost in my mind, and they were what enabled me in 1973 to take that "comedown" job assignment I described in my introduction to this book.

Meanwhile, at home, Audrey found a new kind of husband, one easier to live with. Our house was opened along with our hearts. We ministered to young people with problems and became foster parents to a succession of ten "daughters" who were given a new start in life. And, most enjoyable, the Lord began giving me opportunities to tell others about Him.

Although I had testified in my church, where three people came to Jesus, my ministry got into high gear when I began encouraging others outside of church to commit their lives to Jesus Christ. I did this through speaking before a variety of secular and religious groups. In addition, I am a director-at-large of the Full Gospel Business Men's Fellowship International (a Christian worldwide men's organization) and have helped conduct their Executive Leadership Training Seminars. I also serve on the board of directors of the Episcopal Renewal Ministry.

God also used my conversion experience to help me introduce more than fifty of my fellow insurance workers to Him.

Life has never been more exciting. Even in the difficult times, which we all face in this world, God has been there with me as He promised. He sustained me through a heart attack and, as described earlier, through major bypass surgery. Today, He continues to give me strength.

Once I was a top-notch life insurance salesman. I still feel that life insurance is the best material protection a man can provide for his family.

But today I take great delight in telling people about the greatest "life insurance" of all, spiritual protection. Its benefits are everlasting life, and God provides it absolutely free.

All we have to do is ask for it by admitting that we're imperfect, that we can't do it by ourselves, and then surrendering to His Son, Jesus Christ.

I have met many men and women who are truly successful. Invariably, they have found their power source through God. No matter what they have done in life, how wrong they may have been in the past, God has forgiven them, as He will forgive you.

All it takes is surrender, a complete surrender of oneself to God. It's so simple to do. Turn to our Lord, Jesus Christ, admit you can't do it by yourself, accept His forgiveness, and step out into a brand-new life. In it you will find guidance through the presence of His Holy Spirit, help through other men and women who have surrendered themselves in this manner, and, so important, you will find infallible direction in the Holy Bible.

Read some of it every morning. From my own experience, I can guarantee you that you will find in it inspiration and illumination for the problems, questions, and challenges you will face that day.

God bless you.

Source Notes

How This Book Came About

1. Robert J. Ringer, *Looking Out for Number One* (Beverly Hills, Ca.: Los Angeles Book Corp., 1977), p. 10.
2. Michael Korda, *Success! How Every Man and Woman Can Achieve It* (New York: Random House, Inc., 1977), p. 4.
3. Ibid., p. 5.
4. Ibid.
5. Ibid., p. 13.
6. The *New York Times,* August 19, 1984.

Chapter 1 The Principle of Putting Others First

1. Ecclesiastes 9:10 NEB.
2. Acts 20:35.

Chapter 2 The Principle of Turning the Other Shoulder Blade

1. Matthew 18:15.
2. Matthew 6:12.

Chapter 3 The Principle of Mea Culpa

1. Walter Kiechel III, "When a Manager Stumbles," *Fortune* magazine, November 12, 1984, p. 265.
2. See especially chapter 9, "Sin, So What?" in *Whatever Became of Sin?*, Karl Menninger (New York: Hawthorn Books, Inc., 1973), pp. 173–188.

Chapter 4 The Principle of Relinquishing Worry

1. Adapted from Denis Waitley, *Seeds of Greatness* (Old Tappan, N.J.: Fleming H. Revell Company, 1983), pp. 183, 184.
2. John 14:1 KJV.
3. Proverbs 23:7.

Chapter 5 The Principle of Loyalty

1. Ephesians 6:5–8 KJV.
2. Daniel 1:1–20 KJV.
3. Ecclesiastes 1:9 NEB.

Chapter 6 The Principle of Hanging in There

1. Proverbs 12:15 KJV.

Chapter 7 The Principle of Winning by Losing

1. Exodus 2.
2. Ecclesiastes 9:10 RSV.

Chapter 8 The Principle of Pain as a Blessing

1. "Pain Relief's Founding Father," *Time* magazine, June 11, 1984, p. 65.
2. Max Cleland, *Strong at the Broken Places* (Lincoln, Va.: Chosen Books, 1980).
3. Romans 8:28 KJV.
4. Cleland, *Strong*, pp. 155, 156.

Chapter 9 The Principle of Asking for Help

1. Joshua 3:12–17.

Chapter 10 The Principle of Friendship

1. John 13:34 KJV.

Chapter 12 The Principle of Communicating Your Ideas

1. John T. Molloy, *Molloy's Live for Success* (New York: Bantam Books, 1983), p. 137.
2. Acts 17:16–34 RSV.

Chapter 13 The Principle of Speaking With Authority

1. John T. Molloy, *Molloy's Live for Success* (New York: Bantam Books, 1983), p. 152.
2. Acts 27.
3. Matthew 20:27 NEB.

Chapter 14 The Principle of Family First

1. Denis Waitley, *Seeds of Greatness* (Old Tappan, N.J.: Fleming H. Revell Company, 1983), pp. 213, 214.

Chapter 15 The Principle of Using Your Talents

1. Luke 9:62 RSV.

Chapter 16 The Principle of Surrender

1. Proverbs 3:5 KJV.
2. Proverbs 26:13, 14 KJV.
3. James 4:7 KJV.
4. Nehemiah 1–6.